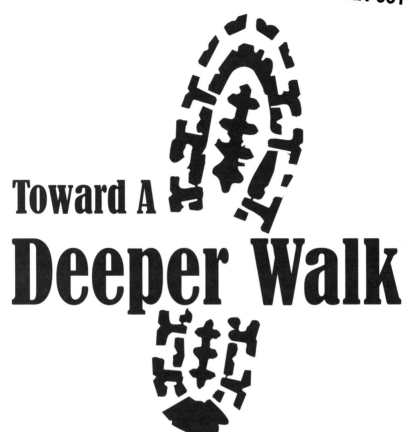

Toward A
Deeper Walk

Toward A Deeper Walk

Heart-focused training
for the journey of life

MARCUS WARNER

Mall Publishing Co.
THE PRINTED WORD THE PLANTED SEED

HIGHLAND PARK, ILLINOIS

Printed in the United States of America

Published by:
Mall Publishing
641 Homewood Avenue
Highland Park, Illinois 60035
1.877.203.2453

Book Design by Marlon B. Villadiego

ISBN 1-934165-18-2

Unless otherwise noted, all scripture quotations are from the New International Version (NIV) of the Holy Bible.

For licensing / copyright information, for additional copies or for use in specialized settings contact:

Marcus Warner

18741 N. Union Street
Westfield, IN 46074
1.317.896.6482
marcus@deeperwalkinternational.org

TABLE OF CONTENTS

HOW TO USE THIS BOOK

Here are some suggestions on how to
use this book for maximum impact.

USING THE BOOK BY YOURSELF

a) Read through the book once

b) Re-read the book chapter by chapter and do the exercises

USING THE BOOK WITH A PARTNER

a) Help each other memorize the verses in the
    spiritual exercises

b) Discuss the starter questions

c) Share portions of your journaling

USING THE BOOK IN A SMALL GROUP

a) Have the leader summarize the teaching from the chapter

b) Use the starter questions to encourage discussion
    (Don't feel like you have to use all of them)

c) Pray for the heart issues that surface during the group time.

d) Resist trying to fix people—especially during group time.
    Stress to participants that the group needs to be a safe place
    to share without fear of condemnation or pat answers to
    heart-level issues.

e) Encourage members to meet with a partner during the week

1 HEART FOCUSED DISCIPLESHIP

I remember sitting on a street corner in Lake Forest, Illinois. It was about midnight. I had been playing basketball with some friends earlier that evening. We were sitting on the curb of a deserted street, still sweaty from the hard play, talking about life. After the others left, I lingered a while longer. I was depressed . . . again. I was in my third year of seminary, preparing to go into ministry. I had attended a private Christian school, graduated from an excellent Bible College, memorized about half of the New Testament, and was nearly finished with my Master of Divinity degree. I was considered a leader in most of the Christian circles in which I moved, but inwardly, I was struggling. I had my good days and my bad days, but overall my Christianity felt like a burden. I was tired of feeling guilty much of the time and knew there had to be more to life than I was experiencing. There were issues in my heart I didn't understand, and no amount of Bible study seemed to fix them. I thought to myself, "If this is all there is to Christianity, maybe I ought to look into something else."

Since that night in Lake Forest, I have come to realize that what was missing in my relationship with God was just that, a relationship. For a variety of reasons, it was difficult for me to shake the image of God as a stern and distant king who was difficult to please. Most of the time I just

1

didn't think about it and tried to do my best, but there were moments, like the one that night, when it all felt like a waste of time. In the years since then God has begun to teach me lessons He has taught many people before me—lessons about living in the Spirit, connecting with my heart, and seeing Him as the source of joy rather than fear. God knew that I had a trained head, but it was time for a trained heart.

This book is for people like me, who often look good on the outside, but who flounder on the inside. It is also for people with broken hearts who are being beaten down by life. I have learned that the victorious, "abundant" life in Christ is not one that is free of battles and baggage. It is about a deepening relationship with the Father and learning to trust His Father's heart for us.

When I first sensed God's call to start Deeper Walk Ministries, I struggled with the fact that I knew I had so far to go in my own journey. I prayed, "Lord, how can I lead a ministry called 'Deeper Walk,' when I am just beginning the journey myself?" His answer seemed clear. "Don't worry about being perfect. Just invite others to join you in the journey." So that is what I am doing; inviting you to join me on a journey of the heart with the goal of moving into a deeper walk with God.

WHAT HEART-FOCUSED DISCIPLESHIP IS NOT

Part of my problem was that even though I had a lot of academic training, I had not had much training on what a walk with God looks like. I had been educated, but not really discipled. My journey is not that different from many who have grown up in the church. The problem is that very few churches practice heart-focused discipleship. Instead, they practice one of four types of discipleship, none of which is bad. They just usually miss the heart. These approaches are: discipleship by osmosis, church-focused discipleship, head-focused discipleship, and behavior-focused discipleship.

1. DISCIPLESHIP BY OSMOSIS. Osmosis is the process by which cells absorb nutrition from other objects in their environment. In school we used to joke that it would be nice to learn subjects by osmosis. That way you could put a text book under your pillow at night, and in the morning the information in it would have been miraculously absorbed into your brain! Wouldn't that be nice! Unfortunately, many churches rely on the mere fact that people attend and participate in the life of the community to make disciples. It usually works like this. If a person attends the church faithfully, that person gets asked to serve. If the person serves faithfully, they get asked to lead. If they lead faithfully, they become elders. In many cases it is possible for a person to become an elder in the church without ever being discipled. Such people learn to fit in with their environment. The end result is assimilation into the Christian culture without any real transformation of the heart. Their journey may begin with a great deal of passion, but in a few years, they settle into a relatively lifeless routine.

2. CHURCH-FOCUSED DISCIPLESHIP. Keeping the ministries of a church running is hard work, and running them with excellence can be exhausting and requires as many volunteers as a church can get. I know, because I was the senior pastor of a heavily program-driven church for seven years. To address this need, many churches provide discipleship training that is largely church-focused, in the sense that it is designed to grow the church and help the individual at the same time. Such discipleship usually stresses membership (commitment to the local body), spiritual gifts (serving in the local body), evangelism (inviting to the local body), and small groups (connecting to the local body). This type of church-focused discipleship is a wonderful process for assimilating people into the community of believers, but it tends to assume that once you are in a small group, you are being discipled. Sadly, this is often not the case, largely because there is no clear vision of a path to spiritual maturity set before the people.

3. HEAD-FOCUSED DISCIPLESHIP. Academic training does not equal discipleship. It is quite easy to go through Bible College or even seminary and not receive anything close to heart-focused discipleship. I'll never forget one of my friends in seminary saying, "I just finished a course on sin and salvation and never learned how to get saved!" The entire class was a discussion of various academic disputes about predestination, original sin, and such things.

This is the testimony of a student that was submitted to my father, Timothy Warner, for a class at Trinity Evangelical Divinity School. He wrote it as part of a critique on Neil Anderson's book *Victory over the Darkness*.

> I have never been discipled, and I have been a Christian for 20 years. Because of not knowing who I am in Christ, I did not know how to walk according to the Spirit. Therefore, I have been living my life according to the flesh while gaining a lot of head knowledge about the Bible and God... I have struggled so long because of my weakness to say no to myself, and I have really been ineffective for Christ. I was always told by those that I opened up to what to do, but it never had any power in my life. I know a lot of theology, and I know everything I should do; but I do not bear much fruit, and I do not love others the way God wants me to. I have prayed a long time that God would show me how to get my head knowledge to my heart, and now He has shown me the way. I feel like a baby Christian because I have to start at the basics again, but I will swallow my pride and learn how to reprogram my faulty ways of thinking. I have grown up with a poor self-esteem, self-condemnation, self-hatred, bitterness, rebellion, perfectionism, anxiety and a weak functional faith...
>
> I had needs that I tried to have fulfilled by lust, pornography, eating, acceptance by others, withdrawal, and facades. My life is filled with hurts, and I have responded to them incorrectly. I used to really struggle because of my view of how God views me. By reading a couple of helpful books on God's grace, I have been freed from the mentality of perfectionism for God's acceptance and love. Yet my life is still powerless because of my faulty patterns of thoughts, many of which are strongholds.

This testimony has been echoed by thousands who have received head-focused rather than heart-focused discipleship.

4. BEHAVIOR-FOCUSED DISCIPLESHIP. The opposite of heart-focused discipleship is behavior-focused discipleship. It tends to fall into the same trap as behavior-focused parenting. It sends a subtle (or not so subtle) message that your value is based on your performance. Behavior-focused parenting teaches children that they are only valued and accepted when they meet expectations. Behavior-focused discipleship makes the same mistake in relationship to God. It presents him as a parent whom we must seek to please in order to earn love and acceptance. This approach to discipleship often promotes a view of God as someone who loves us, but who cannot affirm or accept us because of our behavior.

My dad often uses the four A's to help people understand this concept. He will write the following four words on a piece of paper: Authority, Accountability, Affirmation, Acceptance. Then he will ask: "Do you see God as an authority to whom you are accountable, from whom you seek affirmation and acceptance by your good behavior? Or is it the other way around? Does God accept you in Christ, affirm you as His child, and ask you to be accountable to his authority on that basis?" If the person identifies most strongly with the first pattern, it means they have a behavior-focused view of Christianity.

My dad will tell you that he was raised in a very legalistic form of Christianity. And to his deep regret, in the early years of his parenting he embraced a thoroughly behavior-focused view of life. Only later in life, after the kids were mostly out of the house, did he and my mom embrace a message of grace. As a result this is the brand of discipleship under which I was raised. Because my relationship with God was based on my performance, it was difficult to know when God was angry and when He was happy, which, of course, doesn't do much to inspire intimacy with Him. In fact, a "sacred romance" was the farthest thing from my mind. It sounded mystical and a bit suspicious to me. I tended to treat God as a master in a distant country whom I was trying to please without knowing if I had succeeded.

There was one night in particular when I knelt down to pray that I closed my eyes, and inside my mind I saw two theater masks—the one for comedy with a smiling face and the one for tragedy with a face that looked angry. I stopped my prayer before it had barely begun and said, "Okay God, which face do you have on tonight?" I didn't give Him time to answer because I didn't expect an answer. I just gave up on praying for the night and did something else, like watch TV.

Behavior-focused discipleship tends to reduce all problems to sin. It often implies that there is a right (or biblical) way to do everything and that any other way of doing things is sinful and therefore, is the cause of all our problems. But dealing with sin without dealing with the heart misses the whole point of dealing with sin, which is to protect our relationship with God.

WHAT HEART FOCUSED DISCIPLESHIP IS

Heart-focused discipleship teaches perspectives and practices that lead to intimacy with God, freedom from bondage, and growth in maturity. These perspectives and practices are anchored in grace and emphasize the importance of living in the Spirit with a functional awareness of the spiritual battle that provides the context for our journey.

This book will teach three perspectives and four practices that are essential to a heart-focused walk with God. In keeping with the theme of a deeper walk and to help you remember the principles being taught, each of the perspectives and practices is symbolized by an object related to backpacking. As I write this, I am at a friend's house in Colorado Springs. They have an outstanding view of Pike's Peak from their back yard and later today I plan to take my family hiking at the Garden of the Gods. This is about as adventurous as I get when it comes to hiking—well marked paths, convenient rest stops, in a place of incredible natural beauty. I've got my hiking shirt and my hiking shoes and I'll take a backpack with water and a few other items. It's a beautiful day and it should be a lot of fun. I'm also looking forward to it because I associate going to the mountains with seeking God. It is a great opportunity to let the beauty and grandeur of the surroundings fill my heart with inspiration. It lifts my thoughts to higher things and gets me away from my normal routine where my heart can come alive. That is the idea behind the backpacking analogy in this book. It represents the idea of intentionally breaking from the routine to experience a deeper walk with God. Here is an outline of what lies ahead.

OUTLINE OF THE BOOK

> **Three Perspectives**
>
> S—Sacred Romance
> S—Sovereign Lordship
> S—Spiritual Warfare

> **Four Practices**
>
> S—Seeking God
> L—Listening to God
> O—Obeying God
> W—Watching the Enemy

THREE PERSPECTIVES

Let us begin with a special backpacking shirt. This shirt is special because it has a bull's eye over the heart. The bull's eye is there to remind you that your heart is your target. As the Scriptures say, "Above all else, guard your heart for it is the wellspring of life" (Proverbs 4:23). Your goal is to connect with God at a heart level so that your relationship with Him becomes the center from which your

The bull's eye reminds us that the heart is the target. The three rings represent the three core perspectives.

life flows. The bull's eye is also a reminder that whether you make your heart your target or not, Satan will make it his.

The bull's eye has three circles to represent three essential perspectives for building and maintaining a deeper walk with God: (1) sacred romance, (2) sovereign lordship, and (3) spiritual warfare. What you believe in your heart is crucial to the way you live. As Neil Anderson wrote in *Victory over the Darkness*, "People cannot consistently behave in ways that are inconsistent with the way they perceive themselves." These perspectives need to shape the way we think about God if we want to enjoy our walk with Him.

I often draw the center circle of the three rings in the shape of a heart—to symbolize the idea of a sacred romance. A sacred romance is a metaphor for the reality that God wants you to know Him and love Him and to know how much He loves you. As Paul prayed for the Ephesians, "I pray that you, being rooted and established in love, may have power, together with all the saints, to grasp how wide and long and high and deep is the love of Christ, and to know this love that surpasses knowledge—that you may be filled to the measure of all the fullness of God" (3:18-19).

The middle circle that surrounds the heart represents the second of the three perspectives: the sovereign lordship of God. God is sovereign because God is king. You can trust that your king has good plans for you. The suffering you experience is never the end of the story. In light of eternity, there is always a path through the darkness to a good end.

The outer ring of the target represents perspective three: spiritual warfare. This is the understanding that we live in the context of a war with an enemy who wants to keep us from experiencing a sacred romance and trusting God's sovereign lordship. We will never understand our lives until we see them in terms of the cosmic conflict into which we are born. If we want to live "victorious" Christian lives, we need to learn how to fight the battle for our minds and stand against the enemy. A central part of experiencing a deeper walk with God is the mental picture we have of what God is like and how he sees us. Satan understands this and will do everything he can to steal our faith by distorting these core perspectives.

FOUR PRACTICES

There are four practices that are modeled throughout Scripture by men and women of God who walked closely with Him. These practices grow out of the perspectives symbolized by the target over the heart on the backpacking shirt. They also reinforce these perspectives by introducing disciplines that encourage intimacy in our walk with God.

SEEKING GOD. As we start our journey, we need a backpack. A backpack symbolizes getting away from the normal routine of life to embark on an adventure. You don't wear a backpack to bed. You wear a backpack when you are leaving the suburbs and getting out into nature (unless, of course, you are a student carrying your books to school). A backpack symbolizes adventure and escape from the ordinary in search of a life-giving experience. The Deeper Walk backpack represents the first of four practices that are es-  sential to a heart-focused walk with God. It represents the need to get away from the routines of life and seek God. As we read in Isaiah 55:6, "Seek the LORD while He may be found; call on Him while He is near."

LISTENING TO GOD. Since our goal on this journey is developing intimacy with God, we will put three items into our backpack designed to help us hear His voice. First is a bottle of water to represent fasting. Second is a Bible to represent meditation on God's Word. Third is a journal to record what the Spirit is saying to our hearts. The key idea behind each of these items is "listening.' They represent three practices that can help us develop our ability to listen to the Spirit's voice.

OBEYING GOD. Next we need a walking stick. It will be a large walking stick (as tall as your head) with a handle in the shape of a cross to symbolize the "crucified life" that is to characterize those who follow the Master. The cross also reminds us that every day we face decisions in which we must choose to

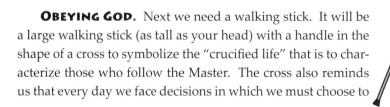

9

crucify the flesh in order to live in the Spirit. In his book *Lifetime Guarantee*, Bill Gilham refers to these daily tests as "mini-crosses." The walking stick reminds us to look for these daily "mini-crosses."

WATCHING GOD (AND SATAN). Finally, we will pack a set of binoculars for our walk. These binoculars aren't just for sight seeing. They  help us look for signs of hope and signs of trouble. Our Deeper Walk binoculars remind us of Christ's words: "Watch and pray so that you will not fall into temptation" (Matthew 26:43). We are to watch for the enemy's strategies that take us captive. Each of us has our own areas of weakness, and the enemy has a specific strategy for attacking us where we are vulnerable. Jesus said that the reason we need to watch and pray is that "the spirit is willing but the flesh is weak." We need to pray that God will show us what we need to do to prepare for the devil's attacks so that on the day of battle we will be able to stand.

SPIRITUAL EXERCISE

The disciples spent three years with Jesus seeing things no one in history had ever seen and hearing things that no one in history had ever heard. In three years, Jesus took the disciples on a journey that revolutionized their outlook on life. It taught them to see life through a different set of lenses than the rest of the world. In the same way, our task is to learn to look at life through kingdom glasses. In the first part of this book we will explore three pillars of a kingdom perspective: the sacred romance (or union with Christ), sovereign Lordship, and spiritual warfare. As we explore these perspectives we will focus on two key questions: How does this perspective help you to see God more clearly, and how does it help you to see yourself more clearly.

Memorize Ezekiel 36:26, "I will give you a new heart and put a new spirit in you; I will remove from you your heart of stone and give you a heart of flesh." The essence of salvation is that we have been born again. To be born again is to be born "from above" by being born of the Spirit. It means that the Holy Spirit has moved into your life so that you have become God's temple. This is who you are, if you are in Christ. God has given you a new heart, and that heart has become the Holy of Holies in which the Spirit lives.

1. As you journal this week, ask God to show you how He sees you.

2. Ask Him for confirmation.

3. Write about what it means to you to have a new heart.

DISCUSSION STARTERS FOR SMALL GROUPS

1. Share your spiritual journey with the group (to the extent that you feel safe doing so).

2. How does your heart feel like a bull's eye? What has Satan done to attack your heart and separate you from God?

3. What would it look like for you to put a bull's eye on your heart this week and give priority to your connection with God?

4. What model of discipleship is most characteristic of your upbringing? How did it help you? How did it affect your view of God and your view of yourself?

5. Thinking of the four A's—authority, accountability, affirmation, acceptance—which order most characterizes your relationship with God? How would life be different if acceptance was the foundation of your walk with God?

2 MATURITY

Jim Wilder defines maturity as acting like yourself. When I first heard that definition, I wasn't sure I liked it. After all, people often use expressions like "I'm just being myself" to justify all sorts of bizarre behavior, whether it is weird hair styles and body art or fits of rage, sexual promiscuity, and drunkenness. We all know that none of these things has anything to do with acting like myself. In fact, such behavior detracts from who I am. It keeps me from being myself, and that is, of course, is Wilder's point. Wearing a mask or playing a role for others to see is the exact opposite of acting like myself. I am acting like myself when I am being the person God created me to be. As a Christian, I am acting like myself when I am living like a saint.

I once had a lady come to me for counseling who had been told all of her life that to be her was to be inadequate. Her mother was a controlling, manipulative, violent woman who made sure her daughters were never an embarrassment to her. The father in this family was passive and lived in fear of his wife. So he just stayed at work most of the time. As I listened to her story unfold it became obvious that she had led a very hard life, drifting from abusive relationship to abusive relationship. Each one reinforced the lie that she was a fundamentally unlovable person. Over time I explained to her that life had trained her to play the role of victim but that this was not her true identity. This lady was a Christian. She was a child of God. At her core she was a good person with a new heart. She was compassionate, generous, witty, and desirable. That was the real her. I don't think I will ever forget the tears in her eyes and the look on her face as she began to understand her only job in life was to act like herself and that acting like herself was a good thing. All of the dysfunctions and emotional baggage she carried with her did not define her: they were the learned responses to a cruel life. They were things that could be stripped away, and when they were, the person she was meant to be would shine through.

Wilder points out that as a Christian, acting like myself means living from the heart Jesus gave me. It is actually the title of his first book, *The Life Model: Living from the Heart Jesus Gave You*. As a Christian, the real you is the new person that you are <u>in Christ</u>. It is your new heart and your new identity in Christ. John Eldredge has rightly pointed out that this new heart is good. It has been circumcised. It is part of the new me that has been made holy and blameless in God's sight. It has been sprinkled clean with the blood of Christ and made holy so that Christ may dwell in our hearts by faith. In this sense it has become the Holy of Holies in the temple of our bodies, in which God's Spirit dwells.

Now the idea that our hearts are good can be troubling because we all know how vile and disgusting our thought life can be and how strong the inner compulsions to evil often are. The temptation is to believe that these depraved tendencies represent "the real me." If you embrace this perspective, it is easy for the enemy to maneuver you into despising yourself and worrying what people would think if they knew "the real you." However, and here we need a really big HOWEVER, Paul clearly teaches that these evil impulses arise not from our new hearts, but from the power of sin that lives in our flesh. He is so adamant about this that he writes of the sins he commits, "so it is *no longer I who do it*, but it is sin living in me" (Romans 7:17). We are not defined by the weakness of our flesh and the power of sin within. These are not "the real me." They are the enemy.

Look at it this way. When you become a Christian, God plants a seed within you. That seed contains all the DNA of the new you. As that seed grows and matures, it transforms you into the likeness of Christ. Your heart is new, but it is untrained. It wants to do what is right, but it needs to learn discernment and discipline. Your good heart is a thing of great potential, like a musical talent that has been given to you by God. The talent is there, but it needs to be developed through training. The goal, however, is not simply discipline. It is the freedom that discipline brings. A truly talented pianist is not one who is merely able to slavishly reproduce the notes on a sheet of music, but the one who makes the music his own and plays from the heart. In the same way the disciplines that train the heart are meant to set us free to be who we really are.

DISCOVERING YOUR TRUE SELF

When I was growing up in the sixties and seventies, it became popular to go off to the mountains or some other exotic location in order to try to "find yourself." Since then it seems that not knowing who I am or what it means to be me has become an epidemic. So much so that most people have abandoned the search, afraid perhaps that there is no answer. But "finding yourself" is not only possible; it is crucial to living a balanced, fulfilling life. This, of course, raises the all important question, "How do you discover your true self?"

Wilder points us in a very helpful direction for discovering what it means to be ourselves. He points us to the idea of satisfaction. Something is satisfying when it leaves you feeling "full" as opposed to addictions and indulgences which leave you feeling empty. Knowing what satisfies is an important part of learning what it means to be you. Closely related to this is the idea of desire. In his book, *The Journey of Desire*, John Eldredge writes that God created us as passionate people who are driven by desire. The key is to learn to discern between desires of the flesh and desires of the heart.

The Bible doesn't talk a lot about satisfaction. But it does talk a lot about what is good. In the beginning, when God made the world and called it "good," He did not mean it was morally good; He meant it was good for us, as John Sailhamer points out in his commentary on Genesis.

The Biblical concept of wisdom centers on this word "good." Wisdom answers the question, "Where do I find what is good?" or "which way to the good life?" The search for wisdom is the search for what is good for me. It is the pursuit of what I desire at the core of my being because it satisfies. Biblical wisdom, as I understand it, has two core elements: discernment, which is the ability to recognize what is good and distinguish it from evil (or what is bad for me); and discipline, which is putting into practice what I know to be good. The wise person is the one who knows what satisfies and is able to distinguish between the good that satisfies and the folly that leaves one empty. The wise person also disciplines himself to say, "No" to what leaves him empty in order to say "Yes" to what satisfies.

Closely related to the word "good" is the word "blessing." Sometimes the word "blessing" is paraphrased "happy." But that can be misleading. To be blessed is to be given what is good or what satisfies. A blessing is a gift. It is something you are given by God as you walk with Him. It is not a reward earned by good behavior, nor is it a destination. A blessing is a by-product that comes from walking with God. One of the ironies of the good life is that you don't get it by seeking it. It is something you get along the way. As Jesus taught, "Seek first His kingdom and His righteousness and all these things will be added to you" (Matthew 6:33).

The word "satisfies" also relates to the idea of passion or desire. One of God's greatest promises is found in Psalm 37:4, "Delight yourself in the Lord and he will give you the desires of your heart." Notice first that God is not anti-desire. God is not a cosmic-killjoy who wants to take away that which brings us joy in order to give us "what is good for us," like a caretaker who refuses us cookies and force feeds us medicine. There may be times when that is exactly what we need, but such moments are temporary. God's heart for us is that we find a deep, abiding joy that makes us fully alive. Second, notice that this blessing is a gift. God gives us the desires of our hearts. It is a gift that comes as we delight ourselves in the Lord. This last part is key. Our walk with God is meant to be a delight. The greatest blessing is the relationship itself. When you are in love with someone, you don't care if you live in a shack or a mansion as long as you are with the one you love. In the same way, God loves to give us good things, but what He wants most is intimacy with Him. If we enjoy God and delight in Him, we will be satisfied regardless of the externals of our daily lives. Yet God's love for us is so deep that He longs for us to experience the fulfillment of our deepest desires in a way that lets us share them together.

Life is meant to be lived with passion in the context of intimacy. It is a shared journey that will take you through many hard times that are designed to strip away that which keeps you from seeing your desires fulfilled and train you in the kind of disciplined walk that leads to fulfilled desire.

The chief enemy of the soul in this regard is temporary indulgence— what the Bible calls "lust." Lust is the desire of the flesh to indulge itself whether that indulgence leads to what is good or not. Look at it this way. A thing is satisfying when it fills you with joy that lasts at least a day or two. On the other hand, temporary indulgences bring a sensation of joy that lasts only as long as the indulgence. When it ends, you often find yourself not only unfulfilled, but emptier than when you started.

The fool lacks the discernment to distinguish between what satisfies and what is merely pleasurable for the moment. But as this person grows in discernment, they begin to discover what fills them up. In so doing, they learn what makes them come alive and what stirs their deepest desires. In the process they discover what it means to be themselves. Thus, the mature person is the one who is developing the discernment and discipline to act like themselves by saying "Yes" to what is truly satisfying at the deepest levels of the heart and "No" to those things that diminish them with cheap indulgences and unsatisfying pursuits.

Eldredge has rightly observed that a significant part of finding what satisfies the deepest longings of our hearts is discovering our role in the larger story of life. We were born for a purpose that is directly related to the deepest desires of our hearts. As we enter into that purpose something in us awakens that makes us feel alive.

Desire, however, cannot be our only guide through life. We have fleshly passions and desires that war against the deep desires of our hearts and the whisperings of the Holy Spirit. But it is not that hard to tell these passions apart. Paul calls the works that flow from the lusts of the flesh "obvious" (Galatians 5:19). The desires of the flesh are fundamentally selfish. They have to do with self-protection, self-promotion, and self-indulgence. The desires of the Spirit are fundamentally loving. They add value to others or they enhance our delight in the Lord.

CHARACTERISTICS OF MATURITY

I had been in ministry for over twenty years when I first came across Jim Wilder's teaching on maturity. It was like someone turned on a light in a dark room and made sense out of my persistent struggles to be the person I knew I had it in me to be. I want to offer a brief summary here of some of the key lessons I have learned as I have begun exploring what maturity is and how you get there.

To help me picture what it means to be mature I have collected a series of characteristics that I remember with the word D.R.E.S.S., as in "this is what it takes to dress for success."

DISCERNMENT. Discernment is the ability to distinguish what satisfies from what leads to emptiness and destruction. Ecclesiastes records Solomon's search for satisfaction. He tried pleasure, knowledge, and achievement, yet it all left him empty. It was like "chasing after the wind." He learned that satisfaction is not found in having more and doing more, but in the gratitude that enjoys all that is good as a gift from God. Soren Kierkegaard serves as an example of the person who learns that there is more to life than the pursuit of pleasure. He wrote in his journal: "I have just come from a party at which I was the soul. Witticism flowed from my mouth and all laughed and admired me. I came home—and here there should be a dash as long as the radius of the earth's circumference—and wanted to shoot myself." Maturity is characterized by the cultivation of an eternal perspective on what satisfies.

RELATIONSHIP. The mature person is able to remain relational even under stress. The immature person sabotages relationships with anger, hypocrisy, withdrawal, and manipulation. One of the phrases Dr. Wilder uses to describe what it means to be mature is "the ability to take care of two people at the same time." This is a hallmark of a responsible person. A mature person is able to find mutually satisfying solutions that create win-win scenarios for the people involved. The immature or childish person cannot do this. They have to take care of themselves first. Only then, if they have the resources left over, will they attempt to take care of someone else. This is one of the reasons so many marriages struggle. Husbands and wives lack the maturity to put the needs of others ahead of their own. Their own lack of joy strength keeps them from nurturing their partner in mutually satisfying ways.

ENDURANCE. James 1:2-4 describes the mature person as one has learned to endure trials with joy. They have learned to suffer well. Mature people are characterized by inner joy that gives them the strength to endure testing. Immature people are consumed by suffering. It defines them and keeps them from acting like themselves. Mature people are characterized by patience, endurance, and long suffering. The source of these virtues is the inner joy that comes from knowing they are loved unconditionally and from the hope that someone who loves them is in control. Unconditional love builds joy strength that gives people what they need to suffer well. This joy strength makes mature people stable and dependable in times of crisis—the sort of person you would want to turn to when you are in trouble.

STRENGTH. A mature person is skilled at living. Such a person loves the process of learning and growing. The immature person despises the disciplines of learning. Their arrogance make them unteachable. I am not saying that people who like to read are good and people who don't are bad. There are all kinds of ways to learn. The point is that the mature person continually expands the set of skills that equip them to handle life. I think of Ben Franklin who taught himself to play the violin at the age of seventy. One of the reasons I admire my parents so much is that I have watched them continue to grow and develop throughout their lives. It keeps them young. My mother, for example, has done intensive counseling with over four hundred women since she reached age sixty-five, even though she had never had any formal counseling training. She even flew to Texas and taught a class for ICBC on issues related to taking women through the Steps to Freedom. She was 82!

SACRIFICE. Strength alone does not make one mature. It is using that strength to serve others that characterizes maturity. Love is the defining mark of maturity. The mature person simply is not consumed with themselves; thus they are free to serve others. The mature person isn't worried about what others think of them. This security allows them to forget about themselves and do what is best for others. If discernment is knowing what is good for me, love is setting aside what is good for me in order to give someone else what is good for them. It is putting someone else's good ahead of your own. This doesn't always mean doing what the other person wants. It means doing what is truly good for them. An alcoholic may want you to enable his or her behavior, but that doesn't mean it is good for them that you do this. Sometimes sacrificing in order to do what is good for someone means having the courage to confront in love or set boundaries that will help the other person and yourself have a healthier relationship in the long run. For the immature person, life is all about me—my rights, my needs, my agenda. They may feel love toward others but find it difficult to demonstrate the type of mature love that does what is good for the other person even at the cost of personal sacrifice.

HOLES IN OUR MATURITY

If you are like me, there are times when you can be very mature and responsible, but there are other times when you are anything but mature. You put yourself first; you expect others to sense what you need and provide it without ever being asked. You fear suffering so much that you will do anything to avoid it. You throw tantrums when you don't get your way. You manipulate and control others out of insecurity and fear that you will not be protected or nurtured if you don't. Most of us, I believe, have holes in our maturity development. These holes are usually directly related to our emotional "buttons." I can go through the day just fine until someone pushes my buttons. Then I suddenly revert into a little child and act like a six-year old.

These holes are not just momentary lapses that come when our buttons get pushed. They are also patterns of fleshly living that we never got under control at an appropriate age. We may lack the ability to get out of bed and set an agenda for our day or fix a budget or establish priorities and stick to them. We may lack skills and disciplines that are necessary for living life well.

Part of overcoming such holes in our maturity is acknowledging that they are there. I often teasingly say that when I got married, "I knew my wife had issues," but I thought I was pretty well adjusted. However, after thirteen years of marriage and finishing what had to be our most difficult year together yet, I came to realize that it was my issues that were sabotaging our marriage, not hers. So, I set out to get help. It was about this time that I cam across Wilder's book *The Life Model* and a counselor who used this book as part of his work. I could see immediately that nearly every problem in my marriage could be traced to holes in my maturity. I just wanted life to be fun. When Brenda didn't cooperate with that agenda, I would get angry. Marriage wasn't supposed to be this hard. I found myself thinking things like, "If she wouldn't be so stubborn and insistent about her agenda, we could be following my agenda and everyone would be happy!" Just recognizing these patterns and talking about them with Brenda has helped immensely.

Beyond recognizing that I had a maturity issue, I have had to commit to counseling and accountability to keep working on the issues that drive my tendencies toward immaturity. As I learned more, I realized that immaturity wasn't only sabotaging my marriage, it was negatively impacting my ministry, and frankly, all my noble pursuits of success.

If you are starting to say to yourself, "Okay, I see that I have holes in my maturity, what do I have to do to fix them?" That's good. The goal of this book is to lay out a path that leads to the greater freedom, intimacy, and maturity that come with a deeper walk. For now, I want to encourage you not to get down on yourself or "beat yourself up" for not being as mature as you wish you were. Jim Wilder once told me that he believes 75% of all males function at an infant level of maturity, which means they don't know what they need or how to ask for it; so they expect others to intuitively recognize what they want and meet their needs. He also estimated that 75% of all females function at a child level of maturity. They know what they want and how to ask for it, but lack the maturity to take care of two people at the same time. I just point this out as a reminder that we are all on a journey. Or as John Eldredge puts it, "we are all unfinished people."

The next chapter looks at the power of perspective. If we are going to grow in maturity we are going to need to develop the perspectives and practices that lead to maturity.

SPIRITUAL EXERCISE

Peter is a model of someone who moved from immaturity to maturity in his walk with God. It wasn't his passion that made him immature. It was his unbelief. Peter grew in maturity as his perspectives changed and he came to see life through kingdom glasses. As his perspectives changed, his practices changed and he grew into a person who lived up to his name, Peter, which means "the rock."

1. In what way do you feel like an unfinished person?

2. What do you see God doing in your life to repair some of the holes in your maturity?

3. When do you find it hardest to act like yourself?

4. Ask the Lord where He wants to start with you this week as you embark on a journey toward maturity.

DISCUSSION STARTERS

1. Who from your past modeled maturity for you? How?

2. What do you think of Wilder's definition of maturity as acting like yourself? Is it helpful to you? How?

3. What did you learn about your own maturity level this week?

4. What impact do you think it would have on your marriage, your parenting, or your other relationships if you could see significant growth in some of these key areas of maturity?

5. What was the most helpful insight for you from this chapter?

3 THE POWER OF PERSPECTIVE

When I was in Little League, I took baseball pretty seriously. I could recite the lineups and key batting statistics of almost every team in the major leagues. I was a big kid and was the dominant player on my team. But, one summer I went into a horrible batting slump. No matter how hard I worked at it, I just couldn't make solid contact with the ball! My dad decided to help me, but not in the way you might expect. He had me listen to a series of cassette tapes by a sports psychologist. This man taught about the importance of visualizing yourself doing things correctly. (For those of you who are concerned at this point, I am not talking about New Age visualization or guided imagery. I am talking about forming a mental picture in your head of hitting a baseball correctly). My dad had me sit in a chair, close my eyes, and try to picture myself hitting the baseball. Now, I had hit hundreds, if not thousands of baseballs in my life, but no matter how hard I tried, I could not picture myself hitting the ball. I missed every time! So, my dad took me outside to a nearby field with a bat and a bucket of balls. He began to pitch to me, but told me not to hit the ball. He didn't even want me to swing at it. He just wanted me to picture myself hitting the ball as it went by. He threw me four, five, six pitches, and each time I pictured myself hitting it. By the sixth or seventh pitch something started to click and I could picture myself hitting a homerun on every pitch. Finally, my dad let me swing. Man, what a difference! I crushed the ball. The next day at the ball park, I hit two home runs and double! Hitting a baseball felt like the easiest thing in the world, because I couldn't picture myself <u>not</u> hitting the ball!

Zig Zigler told the story of a guy who didn't touch a golf club for seven years, and lowered his score by nearly twenty strokes. What was his secret? He had been a prisoner of war who kept himself sane by playing an imaginary round of golf in his mind every day. Each day he played eighteen holes, imagining different weather conditions and different course designs. In meticulous detail he pictured himself hitting each shot flawlessly. After doing this for seven years, he finally got a chance to play a round of golf and lowered his score from the mid-nineties to the mid-seventies without ever practicing.

There is no question that the pictures we rehearse in our minds have the power to mold our performance. Mental pictures about the way life works and the beliefs that are related to them create the filter through which we look at life. They serve as lenses that affect the way we explain and evaluate our experiences. For example, if I have a secular picture of reality, I will not expect to find much activity in the realm of spirits and angels, nor will I value the help that comes from the unseen world. However, if I have a tribal picture of reality, I will then expect to find spirits everywhere and will place great value on making sure I take the necessary steps to gain the help that comes from the world of spirits. This was vividly illustrated by a missionary who told the story of one Amazonian tribe's response to the news that a measles epidemic was making its way from village to village up the river. How would you respond to such news? They responded by cutting the heads off of every rooster in the village. Why? Because they believed that the crowing of the roosters attracted the spirits that caused the measles.

When it comes to the Christian life and experiencing a deeper walk with God, there is virtually nothing more important than the mental picture you have of God, yourself, and the world in which you live. This is your worldview and it will determine how you explain and evaluate life.

It will determine the level of passion you have for knowing God intimately. It will determine the confidence and freedom with which you live and your ability to act like yourself.

Paul understood the importance of our thought life to a successful Christian journey; Malleaf.ai so he writes:

Romans 12:2, Do not conform any longer to the pattern of this world, but be transformed by the <u>renewing of your mind</u>.

Romans 8:5, Those who live according to the flesh have their <u>minds set </u>on what the flesh desires; but those who live according to the Spirit have their <u>minds set </u>on what the Spirit desires.

Philippians 4:8, Finally, brothers, whatever is true, whatever is noble, whatever is right, whatever is pure, whatever is lovely, whatever is admirable—if anything is excellent or praiseworthy—<u>think about such things</u>.

Colossians 3:1-2, Since, then, you have been raised with Christ, set your hearts on things above where Christ is seated at the right hand of God. <u>Set your minds</u> on things above, not on earthly things"

2 Corinthians 4:18, So we <u>fix our eyes</u> not on what is seen, but on what is unseen. For what is seen is temporary, but what is unseen is eternal.

When you think about it; Jesus was an alien. He said so himself. "I am not of this world," he told the Jews. "My kingdom is not of this world," he told Pilate. My point is not that Jesus was an extraterrestrial, but that he saw the world from an alien perspective, as one who was not of this world. Jesus saw life from a kingdom perspective, and he taught his disciples to see life from that same perspective. He taught them that nothing is more important than entering the kingdom. It is worth any price we might be required to pay because nothing in this world can compare with it (Matthew 13:41-42). A kingdom perspective teaches us that we are stewards of the king, charged with investing the resources with which we have been entrusted in kingdom purposes. A kingdom perspective clarifies who we are, why we are here, and what is truly valuable, because it teaches us to think spiritually and eternally.

As Christians, we can live with a mental picture that comes from the

Spirit or one that comes from the flesh. The flesh looks at outward appearances and evaluates things on the basis of self-interest. The Spirit looks at the heart and evaluates everything from a kingdom perspective.

IDENTITY FROM THE FLESH

In his book *The Five Love Languages*, Gary Chapman popularized the idea that you and I are like cars that run on the fuel of love. Our hearts are like big love tanks. When the tank is full, we feel like we can take on the world, but when the tank is empty, we struggle to get out of bed. Early in life children learn what sort of behavior attracts love and acceptance from others and what generally leads to rejection and pain. They learn that the world values things like looks, achievement, status, and talent. The world looks at who we are on the outside and judges us. In the process we begin to develop beliefs about ourselves that stay with us our entire lives. This sense of identity is based on our flesh and what the world says about our flesh, rather than on the truth as God sees it.

Life in the flesh is rooted in comparison. At a very young age people begin to compare themselves with others. Every junior high school (in fact every social circle I have ever been in) has a pecking order that tells you where you rank in comparison to the other people in your group. At the top are the popular kids. They are the best looking or most athletic or have the most money, like the old Billy Joel tune says, "Have you heard about the new fashion, honey. All it takes is looks and a whole lot of money." In the middle of the pecking order are "normal" kids who excel in areas that don't necessarily lead to popularity—like non-varsity sports or chemistry. They may love to read or write stories. They may excel in gardening or music. But because their areas of strength are not the ones the world values, they are considered a notch below the "in crowd". At the bottom of the pecking order are people the world calls "losers." These are the people whose lives seem to be characterized by failure and trouble. They don't compare well with others in those areas the world deems important. As most of us have learned, these pecking orders are completely artificial structures by which the world seeks to define you. Some people never recover from the damage done by this system. Others learn, often with great difficulty, to break away from the system and find value in themselves that is completely unrelated to what the world says about them.

Life in the flesh is a constant roller coaster ride of comparison and introspection. We not only judge ourselves, we judge others and tend to treat them better or worse depending on how we rank them. The result is that we define ourselves and others by comparing our flesh with theirs. In the process we learn to live with a mirror in front of our face, so that we are always either picking at ourselves or admiring ourselves. The result is that we swing back and forth between inferiority and conceit. It is an exhausting, demoralizing way to live, no matter where you are in the pecking order.

I once saw a picture of a famous actress on a magazine cover and the lady next to me said, "She's a real BLT!" I must have had a puzzled look on my face, because to me a BLT was a bacon, lettuce and tomato sandwich! But she explained, "You know, a BLT—brains, looks, and talent." It was a classic example of how the world likes to label people by what they see on the outside. I couldn't help but wonder if that actress had ever cried herself to sleep at night or contemplated suicide over the feeling that who she was on the inside didn't measure up to what she was on the outside. Nobody wins the flesh game. It doesn't matter how talented, beautiful, or famous you are. If your identity and your worth are based on these things, they are fleeting at best. You can still wake up in the morning and believe the world would be better off without you.

IDENTITY FROM THE SPIRIT

What we try to gain from all of our striving in the flesh is something that cannot be earned. It cannot be bought, it cannot be awarded, it cannot be stolen, and we cannot live without it. The "it" to which I refer is unconditional love. By its very nature, unconditional love is being valued regardless of your looks, talent, status or performance. There is no prior condition that must be met before it is received. My friend Jeff Pokone, a pastoral counselor, defines unconditional love as the freedom to fail and still know that you are loved. Take a moment and reflect on that. What difference would it make to you to know you could fail and still be loved? Would you be more daring? Would you take more risks and live with greater freedom?

The love you receive when you fail teaches you that your value lies within—that you are important and worth loving just because of who you are. When failure brings rejection, you learn exactly the opposite. Your heart learns the lie that your worth is determined by your performance—that love must be earned. What a crushing blow to a child's heart! How horrible to go through life believing that you have no intrinsic value and that the only thing that matters is your behavior and achievement.

Our Father in heaven loves us unconditionally. This is what Paul wrote, "God demonstrates His love for us in this: while we were yet sinners, Christ died for us" (Romans 5:8). Christ did not die for the beautiful or the popular or the righteous. Christ died for failures. If you are relying on anything other than Christ's death for your status with God, you are standing on shaky ground, regardless of your position in the world's pecking order. Paul wrote,

> Brothers, think of what you were when you were called. Not many of you were wise by human standards; not many were influential; not many were of noble birth. But God chose the foolish things of the world to shame the wise; God chose the weak things of the world to shame the strong. He chose the lowly things of this world and the despised things—and the things that are not—to nullify the things that are, so that no one may boast before him (1 Corinthians 1:26-29).

It was unconditional love that led God to provide salvation to all people as a free gift. Those who receive that gift enter into His love. God does not hate unbelievers. On the contrary, the Bible says that "God so loved the world." The problem is that unbelievers have ignored and rejected God's love by rejecting His Son's sacrifice on their behalf. They have not entered into that wonderful gift. The sad thing is that many Christians who have received this gift still live as if God's love must be earned. They have put their faith in Christ and are trying to be good, but they do not know how to enter into God's love and live with a clear mental picture of a God who considers them the apple of His eye.

How clear is the picture in your mind of a God who loves you even when you fail? If the picture is fuzzy, or if you have a very different picture of God in your mind, there is a good chance that God's love does not feel very real to you. There is also a very good chance that you have not experienced much unconditional love in your life.

Can you remember a time in your life when you failed and someone made you feel that you were still loved and highly valued? I recently asked that question of a man in his fifties with a wife and three kids. He sat in silence for a few minutes, before I said, "You can't remember a time when you were loved unconditionally can you?" He started to weep. The man had come to see me because he was struggling with paralyzing fear and depression. At the source of his problem was a pair of lies that held him in chains. The first was the belief that the only love available to him was a love that had to be earned. The second was the lie that he was an utter failure. He had recently been fired and had a history of business and social failures. We began to pray and ask God questions. As we did, God began to speak. He spoke gently to the man's heart of his love for him, and told him that his failures did not define him. Before he left, the man's perspective on life had changed and there was actually a smile on his face.

This is the power of perspective. In the chapters ahead we will take a closer look at three crucial perspectives that have the power to change your life. They are perspectives that teach us about who we are, who God is, and what the devil is doing to try to blind us to the truth. These perspectives are the sacred romance, sovereign lordship, and spiritual warfare.

SPIRITUAL EXERCISE

The book of Revelation might well be titled "Visions beyond the Veil." It is as if someone pulled back the curtains to give us a glimpse of the world behind the world. It is instructive to observe that three of the core themes emphasized by this unveiling are sacred romance, sovereign lordship, and spiritual warfare.

1) Sacred Romance. The climactic event of history is the return of the groom for the bride and the celebration of the wedding feast of the

Lamb. Indeed, the battle that is revealed is a battle of a hero against a villain to rescue the damsel in distress.

2) Sovereign Lordship. Throughout the book of Revelation nothing happens on earth that is not initiated in heaven. A seal is opened in heaven and disaster strikes the earth. An angel blows a trumpet, makes a proclamation, or empties a bowl and the earth feels the consequences. The book itself is partially structured by the opening of seals that reveal God's sovereign decrees of the events that bring this age to an end and bring the sacred romance to its fulfillment.

3) Spiritual Warfare. Nowhere in the Bible do we get a more focused look at the role of demons and angels in the lives of those on earth. We see the dragon wage war on the saints. We see the great seductress Babylon and a variety of demonic spirits and strategies for overcoming God's people.

As you reflect on these themes in Revelation, how closely would you say your worldview reflects the one related there? What would change in your life if your perspective was more fully shaped by these themes? Ask the Lord to bring to your mind one perspective He would like to make more real to you. Is there something in the way you think about reality that He wants to change? What difference would it make, if you did?

DISCUSSION STARTERS FOR SMALL GROUPS

1. What role has the power of perspective played in your life?

2. What questions did this chapter raise for you?

3. Give an example of a time when you saw unconditional love at work.

4. What are the consequences in a person's life when unconditional love is missing?

5. How would you describe the mental picture you have of God? Of yourself?

4 PERSPECTIVE 1: SACRED ROMANCE

One of our family's favorite movies is *Pride and Prejudice*. It is the story of a young woman named Elizabeth (Lizzie) Bennett and her relationship with the mysterious Mr. Darcy. At first Darcy appears cold and aloof. He even snubs Elizabeth at a local dance and, in general, creates a very bad first impression. To make matters worse, an acquaintance of Mr. Darcy tells Lizzie a story that convinces her Mr. Darcy is a loathsome man. While the young lady's impression of the aristocratic Darcy is going from bad to worse, the man himself is falling hopelessly in love with her. Unaware of her beliefs about him, Darcy proposes. Stunned, Lizzie flatly rejects him with the unkindest of words. Yet, as the story progresses, things begin to change. Elizabeth begins to see Mr. Darcy in a different light. She learns that the stories she was told are not true and that he is, in fact, the most noble, admirable, amazing man she has ever met. A series of events brings her into Mr. Darcy's world, and she is able to see him as he really is. In the end, she falls completely in love with him and, of course, they live happily ever after.

For many of us, God is like Mr. Darcy. Even though He is everything we could ever hope for, we see Him through eyes that have been distorted by his enemy's lies. Our misguided views of what He is like pour water on the flames of our passion. We may honor Him with the duty owed to a superior, but we feel no real passion for intimacy with him. Your view of God may not be as distorted as what I have described, but the reality is that most of us have doubts about God at the heart level that hinder our desire for Him. One of the central goals of a heart-focused journey is to develop a mental image of God as someone we not only serve, but someone we actually like!

THE LOVER LORD

A few years ago someone gave me a set of sermons delivered by Joseph Tson at the 2004 ICBC conference in Sioux City, Iowa. I have heard a lot of sermons in my life, but these had a profound impact on me. In fact, the outline of this book is partly indebted to those sermons. Dr. Tson was a pastor in Romania who was persecuted for his faith by the KGB. He has a dramatic testimony of walking with God through that experience, and I will share a few of those stories in the next chapter. At one point in his journey, Dr. Tson was at Oxford University where he had the privilege of sitting under the teaching of Dr. Martin Lloyd-Jones. Lloyd-Jones stressed time and again that the central pillar of Christian thought is the sovereignty of God. Dr. Tson expressed his gratitude for the emphasis on God's sovereignty because it is an extremely important perspective in our Christian journey. However, Dr. Tson argued that there is a pillar even more fundamental than sovereignty--one that sets Christianity apart from all other faiths. That pillar is something known to generations of believers as "union with Christ." The Bible refers to this as "abiding in Christ." John Eldredge calls it "The Sacred Romance." It is an intimate relationship with Christ in which we tune our hearts to the voice of the Spirit. It is a walk with Christ characterized by seeking, listening, and obeying that leads **to** a life that is centered in Christ and lived from the inside out.

In one of his sermons, Joseph Tson illustrated the nature of this sacred romance with a story by the Danish philosopher Soren Kierkegaard called "The King who loved a Humble Maiden." I want to share my own version of that story with you here.

There was once a young king who was handsome and charming with more wealth and power than anyone in the kingdom. Based on his position he knew there wasn't a woman in the kingdom who would refuse him if he asked her to marry him. Thus, he would never know if she really loved him or if she married from obligation or the benefits she stood to gain. He wanted to marry for love, so he devised a plan. He went out among the people disguised as a commoner.

Upon entering a certain village, he met a beautiful girl of uncommon character with a delightful personality. As soon as he met her, he knew in his heart that she was the one for him. He noticed that her family had money and that they also needed some carpentry work done; so, the next day he strolled into town with the tools of a carpenter bundled in a sack that he slung over his shoulder. He went to the town square and began calling out, "Carpenter for hire, carpenter for hire!" As he had hoped, the girl's family hired him and he began to mend their broken items. Day after day he came to work in their home. At first the young woman paid little attention to him, but in time she began to notice that he carried himself differently than the other young men she knew. He was always courteous. He did his work well and there was a quiet dignity about him she found attractive. Sometimes she brought him something to drink or found some other reason to interact with him, and before long she was looking forward to their meetings. One day he invited her to take a walk with him after work; and soon a romance was blooming.

Her parents were none too happy about this. They were people of means in a small town, and this carpenter boy, though gracious and handsome, was obviously poor, and who knew who his parents were! But the girl was adamant. "I love him," she said, "and if he asks me, I plan to marry him!" The young man overheard the conversation and knew the time had come to reveal his true identity.

The next day news began to spread through town that the king was coming to visit their small village. People began cleaning their shops and decorating the town square. The mayor prepared a speech and a banner was hung welcoming the king to their humble town. Sure enough, just before noon on the following day, the king's carriage arrived with a company of soldiers in dress uniforms. It was quite a spectacle, for the king was very rich. As the carriage rumbled to a stop, people waited with baited breath to see what would happen next. A footman climbed from the carriage and began walking toward the assembly. There was an audible gasp in the crowd as the footman knelt before the young carpenter and said, "Your majesty, I have come to take you back to the palace." A buzz spread through the crowd as, one by one, the people began to kneel in his presence. Soon, he was the only one left standing. Looking around at the scene before him, the king spotted the one he loved. Walking toward her, he helped her to her feet and then . . . he knelt before her. "I am sorry to have misled you," he said, "but I had to know that you loved me for who I was and not for my crown. My beloved, will you marry me and become my queen?" In utter disbelief, she jumped into his arms, and he began to twirl her around and around. The towns folk cheered, "Long live the king! Long live the king!" as the happy couple climbed into the carriage, and headed toward the palace where, of course, they lived happily ever after.

This story embodies God's heart toward us. John Eldredge writes of Kierkegaard's story, "The king clothes himself as a beggar and renounces his throne in order to win her hand. The Incarnation, the life and death of Jesus, answers once and for all the question, 'What is God's heart toward me?'"[1] This is vitally important because it is in God's heart toward me that I learn who I really am.

In Zechariah 2:8, God calls His people "the apple of His eye." I love this expression. To be the apple of someone's eye is to be the reason for the twinkle in their eye. You see it when a baby locks eyes with someone smiling at them. The smiling face turns on the "joy juice" in the baby's brain, and you can see the joy all over their face. It can be hard to believe, but the thought of you makes God smile!

GRACE

The sacred romance we are invited to enjoy is rooted in grace. The opposite of grace is law. Under law I seek to earn acceptance and blessing from God by my obedience to his commands. The Law, however, is

1. John Eldredge, *The Sacred Romance*,

hollow. It commands an outward conformance to a set lifestyle, but it can do nothing about my heart. This was the problem with the pharisaic Judaism of Christ's day. The Pharisees looked good on the outside and were diligent about all those things that set them apart as Jews. But their faith was hollow. Inwardly, they were filled with darkness and corruption. Jesus exposed this hypocrisy and the futility of their religion in much of his teaching. Jesus was far more radical than most of us realize. His teachings, and ultimately his death and resurrection, destroyed the external religion of the Jews and replaced it with a religion of the heart. It brought an end to the externals of circumcision, Sabbath observance, tithing, and temple worship. It brought an end to the law so that our walk with God would not be weighed down by the external demands of the law in order that we might be set free to live from the heart. It replaced the external motivation of the law with the internal motivation of a love relationship with the King that makes us want to obey Him. This is the new covenant faith—a law written on the heart through the indwelling presence of the Spirit of God.

One of the greatest tragedies in the church today is the re-creation of a religion of externals that misses the heart. Grace removes the Law so that we may have a heart-focused walk with God that is rooted in the unshakable foundation of the finished work of Christ and guided by the indwelling presence of God's Spirit.

THE FINISHED WORK OF CHRIST

As Jesus died on the cross he uttered a single word in Greek with profound implications for the God's relationship with His creation: "*tetelestai*"—"it is finished." Jesus fulfilled the law with his life and destroyed it with his death. Paul wrote, "[Christ abolished] in his flesh the law with its commandments and regulations" (Ephesians 2:15). The finished work of Christ finished the Law. It ended that covenant and established a new covenant. This new covenant replaces law with grace and gives us a new identity. The author of Hebrews put it this way, "We have been made holy (i.e., we have become saints) through the sacrifice of the body of Jesus Christ once for all" (10:10). The new covenant gives us a new identity that opens the door to intimacy with God. Consider these words from Hebrews 10:19-22, "Therefore, brothers, since we have confidence to enter the Most Holy Place by the blood of Jesus, . . . let us draw near to God with a sincere heart in full assurance of faith." Notice: (1) Entering the Most Holy Place means entering the presence of God. Christ's finished work opens the door to intimacy with God. (2) We are now free to draw near to God without ceremony or sacrifice (3) God's desire is not outward show, but the sincerity of a heart that is devoted to Him. He desires a heart-level relationship. (4) Our assurance that God will accept us is based on faith in the sufficiency of the finished work of Christ. To put all of this as plainly as I can: Christ died so we could experience intimacy with God. He removed the law and removed our guilt. He removed the necessity for sacrifice and the need for ceremony. In its place he made a way into the very presence of God. When we participate in the New Covenant, we stand before God as beloved children, cleansed, forgiven, and accepted because of the finished work of Christ.

Now that grace has replaced the Law, we need to be careful not to return to the Law by rebuilding a series of external standards by which we measure our acceptance to God. God is not interested in the externals except as they reflect the heart. Even in the Old Testament we are told that "man looks at the outward appearance, but the Lord looks at the heart" (1 Samuel 16:7). Now He is especially interested in the new heart that He gave us, and He wants us to draw near to Him again and again—free from the fear of condemnation and anger. He got rid of the Law so we would be free to pursue intimacy with Him. He did not get rid of the Law so we could indulge our fleshly appetites for worldly pleasures. That would mean He set us free in order to move away from intimacy. God replaced the Law with grace so we would be free to pursue a sacred romance with the one whose love for us is immeasurable.

FREE TO FAIL

A crucial aspect of the sacred romance God wants us to enjoy is embodied in the word grace. Grace is essentially God's unconditional love toward us. As we saw in the last chapter, it is the freedom to fail and still be loved. God's love for us is not rooted in our performance. It is not conditional upon our success or failure in living the Christian life. God doesn't want us to try to please Him by performing for Him in order to earn His acceptance. Such a perspective leads to introspection and a tendency to see everything that might possibly be wrong with us. God wants us to rest in the knowledge that we are free to fail and still be loved. Indeed, sometimes God may want us to fail, if for no other reason than to learn that we can fail and still be loved.

The movie *Elizabethtown* is about a young man named Drew who fails horrifically. He launches an initiative at a major shoe company that costs them nearly one billion dollars. He is so devastated by the implications of his failure that he arrives at his apartment that night determined to kill himself. Providentially, his plans are interrupted by a phone call telling him that his estranged father has died and that his rather dysfunctional family needs him to represent them at the funeral and handle the crisis for them. This turn of events distracts him from his morbid task long enough for him to catch a plane from the Pacific Northwest to Louisville, Kentucky so that he can attend his father's funeral. On the flight he meets Claire, a flight attendant with an irrepressively positive outlook on life. Fate seems destined to bring them together as in the course of the next few days, their paths cross several times and they begin to fall in love. In one of the turning points of the story, Drew feels compelled to reveal the dark secret of his monumental failure to Claire. He is convinced that for the rest of his life his name will be synonymous with failure to millions around the world. He is also pretty sure that this confession will be the end of their relationship. Instead, this is what Claire said: "So you failed. You failed, you failed, you failed . . . You failed. You failed, you failed, you failed . . . so what?" She didn't make excuses for him. She didn't pretend it wasn't a huge failure. She called it what it was . . . but she also made it perfectly clear that she loved him anyway. The question was, "Would he accept her love? Would he allow himself to be loved in spite of his failure?" Isn't this the question we all face in one way or another? It is the question of grace: "Will we let God love us in spite of our failure?"

Being free to fail does not perpetuate a culture of failure. On the contrary, it creates an atmosphere of confidence that encourages success.

When you are not afraid to fail, you are free to be more courageous. You are free to dream and explore life's possibilities. I have been told that President George W. Bush credits the secret of his success to the fact that as a child, he was given the freedom to fail and still know that he was valued and accepted. I cannot tell you how important this is.

ABIDING IN CHRIST

Grace does not change the fact that some of the things you are free to do are stupid, even sinful. There is still such a thing as wisdom. Paul put it this way, "All things are lawful for me, but not everything is beneficial" (1 Corinthians 10:8). Grace does not remove the tangible consequences of sin. You may be free to eat junk food, but it doesn't mean the junk food won't negatively affect your health. You may be free to do foolish things, but it doesn't mean that your foolishness will not create problems. Because of grace, however, you will always be loved, and you will not be alone in your problems. Because of grace, you will have a loving Father at your side who wants to rebuild your confidence and help you move forward again.

The hard part for us is embracing God's grace. It is allowing ourselves to accept it. Some of us hold on to our failures so tightly and fear God's displeasure so intensely that we cannot forgive ourselves. It prevents us from receiving God's grace and taking the faltering steps forward that will return us to the pathway of hope. This is what it means to rest in God's love. This is what it means to abide in Christ. It is allowing Christ to love you, and letting his love for you fill your heart so that you live life with confidence and freedom.

Read John 15 again and notice the descriptions Jesus gives of what it means to abide in him. We abide in Christ when his *words* abide in us (v 7), when we abide in his *love* (v 9), and when we *obey* his commandments (v 10). The order here is significant. His words to us tell us that he loves us. We abide in him when we trust his love and receive it. Once we know that we are loved and receive that love we are ready to gladly obey his commandments and to show that same love to others. To abide in Christ is to live in the knowledge of his unconditional love toward us so that his love may flow through us into the lives of others, bearing much fruit (v. 5), bringing God glory (v. 8), and filling our hearts with joy (v. 11)!

One of the ways we receive God's love is by forgiving ourselves for our failures. Forgiving yourself is not excusing yourself. It is not being easy on yourself. And it will not remove other consequences that have occurred because of your sin. Forgiving yourself begins with admitting that what you have done is wrong. You must first confess your sin as sin. The process is not complete, however, until you choose to receive God's forgiveness, so that at a heart level you truly believe that you are forgiven. This is more than confessing sin. It is believing that 1 John 1:9 means what it says—God is faithful to forgive our sin when we confess it, and it is receiving by faith the forgiveness for that sin that allows you to move forward once again and to live without condemnation (Romans 8:1).

The key to living in grace is meditation on the truths that reinforce a grace perspective. In this way we let the words of Christ abide in us in a way that helps us to abide in his love and share that love with others.

CONCLUSION

The two most important perspectives of a sacred romance are the way you see God and the way you see yourself. These are Satan's two greatest targets. If he can distort the way you see God, he can distort the way you see yourself, and the result is a loss of intimacy. You could say that the secret of the Christian life is your view of God. As you grasp how wide and long and high and deep the love of God for you is, everything else falls into place. Because our enemy understands this, he throws everything he has into distorting our view of God.

This chapter introduced the importance of seeing God's love for you. In the next chapter we will look at the second core perspective of a kingdom worldview; the importance of trusting God's sovereign work in your life.

SPIRITUAL EXERCISE

Perhaps the most dramatic perspective change in the Bible was the one that led the Pharisee persecutor of the church, Saul of Tarsus, to become Paul, the apostle to the Gentiles and defender of the faith. At the heart of his transformation was a dramatic change in his view of God that radically altered the way he saw himself and the world around him. (Read about it in Acts 26). In his letter to the Ephesians, Paul wrote hat his prayer for them was that "the eyes of their hearts" would be opened. He wanted them to have a perspective change. Specifically, he wanted them to grasp how wide and long and high and deep the love of Christ for them was and to begin to grasp all the ways in which they had been blessed in Christ.

1. What would change in your life if you were to encounter the risen Christ? How do you think it would impact your view of God and of yourself?

2. As you journal this week, ask God to show you how He sees you. Ask Him for confirmation.

3. What are the obstacles that make it hard for you to receive love?

4. Ask the Lord what needs to be done to overcome those obstacles?

DISCUSSION STARTERS FOR SMALL GROUPS

1. Which story had the biggest impact on you? Why?

2. What insights did you sense the Spirit giving you as you read this chapter?

3. What questions did your reading raise for you?

4. How have you experienced God's pursuit of your heart?

5. How have you tended to respond to that pursuit?

6. How would you describe your view of God?

7. How do you think life would be different if you wore kingdom glasses all the time?

5 PERSPECTIVE 2: SOVEREIGN LORDSHIP

Let's make one thing clear up front. Sovereignty does not mean determinism. We do not live in *The Matrix*. God did not write a software program for the universe that creates the illusion of free will while actually predetermining everything that happens. Such a view of reality flies in the face of the entire message of the Bible that life is about love—receiving it freely and giving it freely to others. That having been said, we are not forced to the other extreme of a world in which God is essentially an observer waiting to see what we will do and hoping for the best. Instead, the Bible portrays a fairly clear picture of a world in which God is king. He makes decrees and initiates activity at both the cosmic and the individual level. It presents God as the initiator of a great purpose for the world and the provider for even the smallest details of our lives.

The goal of this chapter is not to solve every mystery related to the unseen interplay between God's free will and man's, but to develop a mental picture of God as someone you trust. We will do this in two ways. First, we will explore the idea of God as the divine chess player. Second, we will look at the death and resurrection of Jesus as a model of how sovereignty works.

THE COSMIC CHESS PLAYER

Several years ago I was introduced to the idea of God as the divine chess player, and it has helped me think about the way God's sovereignty operates. If you think of your life as a game of chess, it often appears to be played on a sixty-four square chess board. You make your moves and observe the moves of others and may get pretty good at playing the game. After a while, you can start to think that you don't need any help playing this game or that you have a pretty good handle on how the game is unfolding. What you don't see, is that your sixty-four square playing surface is only a small part of a much larger playing surface that is miles wide and multiple levels deep. In realms you cannot see, God is playing an unbelievably complex game of which we only get momentary glimpses. Any sense that you are in control of your life is pure illusion. This game is far too complex for any of us to understand completely; so God tries to make it simple for us. He says, "Trust me."

God has intentionally designed the game of life in such a way that we have to live by faith. The world is too complex to ever understand it all. Whether it is the microscopic world of electrons and DNA, the utter vastness of the universe, the complexity of the human body, or the unseen realm of spirits, there is simply too much for anyone to say, "I have it all figured out. There is nothing I do not understand!" Whether you believe in God or not, you live by faith. This is not because faith is blind or irrational; but because faith, by definition, relates to what you cannot see and cannot prove. So why did God design the world like this? I believe it is because faith relates to what is in the heart and not just to what is in the head. The mind can make a case for whatever it wants to believe, but the heart will ultimately take us to its own destination.

The doctrine of sovereignty asks us to trust God in the same way that a child instinctively trusts a parent. (Granted, parents often violate that trust and lose it, but that does not mean that children do not at least start out trusting their parents). This kind of faith does not anxiously try to figure out what God is up to, then having "figured it all out" decide, "Okay, I see what God is up to so I'll choose to trust Him." This kind of faith trusts God because of who He is regardless of what things look like. I must confess that I have spent a lot of my life pursuing the wrong kind of faith. Instead of trusting God to be good and to work all things together for good, I struggled to determine what His plans were and then decided if I was okay with that. I wrestled with God for control of my life because I didn't trust Him to exercise His sovereign lordship in a way that wouldn't lead to pain and disaster.

THE CRUCIFIXION AND THE PROBLEM OF EVIL

While teaching a Sunday School class recently, someone asked me to explain why bad things happen to good people. This is the fundamental question that every religion must answer, "How do we explain the presence of suffering and evil?" Buddhism teaches people how to die to the desires that cause suffering. Hinduism blames suffering on the karma of a past life. Islam teaches submission to suffering as part of submission to the will of Allah. Christianity roots our understanding of suffering in God's passionate love. God is love and He wants to share that love with us. He wants us to love Him. But He cannot force us to love Him—that would defeat the whole purpose. If you wanted someone to fall in love with you, and you hypnotized them in order to make that happen, you might enjoy your "romance" for a while, but sooner or later you would want to ask, "If they had a free choice, would they still choose me?" God so valued love that He bestowed upon humans a measure of freedom. There are many areas in which we do not have free will. We can't choose our parents, our race, our backgrounds, etc. We can't live beyond the capacity of the minds and bodies we have been given. And there are many other ways in which our freedom can be limited by the circumstances of life. God uses all of these limitations along with His own free choices to draw us to Himself and play an active role in our lives. He is not to blame for the existence of evil, but in determining that there would be free will, God knew that there would be evil. He knew that one of the consequences of His decision was that evil would come into existence and that tremendous suffering would result. Even so God believed that love was worth it. This interplay between the cost of love and God's sovereignty can be clearly seen in the story of the death and resurrection of Christ.

Several years ago I heard a sermon on tape (I can't remember who the preacher was), that explained the sovereignty of God and its implications for the problem of evil by explaining three principles that can be seen in the death and resurrection of Jesus: (1) God permits evil;(2) God uses evil; and (3) God overcomes evil.

GOD PERMITS EVIL. God sent Jesus to the cross. He didn't simply permit it. He sent Jesus into the world for the express purpose of dying on the cross. It was God's will for Jesus to suffer. I envision a dialogue something like this.

"Son"

"Yes, Father"

"There is something I must ask you to do, and it is breaking my heart to ask you to do it."

"What is it, Abba?"

"There is only one way to reclaim the evil done by the great deceiver and the evil done by humans. You must enter the realm of darkness as a human. You must endure the ignorance, evil, arrogance, and stupidity of worthless people, who think they are better than you. You must teach people the truth. Show them a better way. Shine as a light in the darkness and then . . . I wish there was another way, my Son . . . you must die at their hands. For twenty four hours you will be in their power, and they will do to you whatever they wish and then they will kill you. In that hour, I will have to turn my back on you."

GOD USES EVIL. God could have ended the conversation there. He could have said, "I am king. I have spoken. Now go." As the sovereign, He has the power to decree whatever He pleases (Psalm 115:1). But there is more to this picture. God only permits evil that He can use to bring about a greater good in the end. Taken as the illustration it is, perhaps the rest of the conversation looked something like this.

"Abba, why would you choose to place me in the hands of evil? What do you gain from this?"

""You know that I would never decree evil for you – unless it could be used for a greater good and unless I could overcome the evil in the end. I have decreed this not just because it will bring me glory, but because of what it will do for you, and especially for my children, the sons and daughters of man. You will be the sacrifice that makes atonement for their sin. Your blood will sprinkle them and make them clean so that we may dwell with them and they with us. It will sanctify them and make them holy. Your blood will establish a new covenant that will endure forever by which mankind may enter into our love and receive forgiveness for sins. Your death will pay the ransom for our captive children. It will redeem them from their slavery. It will satisfy the demands of the Law, ending forever the curse against them. It will purchase salvation for all who believe."

"Then, Father, not my will but yours be done."

Just as God decreed suffering for Jesus, He decrees suffering for us. He does not cause the suffering. The suffering is caused by the devil and the children of darkness. God is like a general sending troops into battle knowing some will die, some will be wounded, and some will be captured. It is not His desire that this happen, but in a world at war, for the greater good, He must issue decrees that result in suffering, even though it breaks His enormously good and loving heart. Sometimes God does this in response to choices we have made that open the door to Satan's work. Sometimes He does this in response to the choices that others have made. And sometimes He does this simply because He knows it is the only doorway to some greater good.

The trials we face in this life are meant to tear us down in order to build us back up. Satan intends them for our destruction. God intends them for our benefit. It is painful at the time, but the eternal results it produces far outweigh the temporary suffering it requires.

GOD OVERCOMES EVIL. Christ's story did not end at the cross. His suffering was not the end of the story. God raised Jesus from the dead. He exalted Him to His own right hand and gave Him a name above every name, so that at the name of Jesus every knee shall bow. In this way God overcame the evil of the crucifixion.

God's victory over evil means that we can live with hope. Paul often referred to the message he preached as a gospel of hope. As Christians, the lives we live in this world are anchored in the reality of all that Jesus accomplished by His death and resurrection. Though we are in the world, we are not of the world. Though we will suffer in this life and experience the same rejection and the same arrogant treatment as Jesus, we can take heart in knowing that Jesus has overcome the world (John 16:33). It will often appear that Satan is winning, just as it appeared that he had won when he crucified Christ. It will often feel like evil has all of the power, just as it looked to some as if Jesus stood helpless before Pilate and the Sanhedrin. But such a perspective would be tragically misguided. As Jesus told Pilate, "You would have no authority over me, if it were not given to you from above" (John 19:11). There is no power we face, no evil we endure that is not permitted, that cannot be used for a greater good, and that cannot be overcome in the end.

Could there be a greater evil than the crucifixion of the Son of God? If God permitted this evil, used it, and overcame it, is there any evil He cannot use and overcome? John R. W. Stott wrote: "I could never myself believe in God if it were not for the cross. In the real world of pain, how could one worship a God who was immune to it? The only God I believe in is the one Nietzsche ridiculed as 'God on the cross,' That is the God for me!" (*The Cross of Christ*, 335-336).

In an article titled "Robin Williams and the Problem of Suffering," John Bowen offers the following insight:

> After my wife Deborah had been in the hospital, near death, some years back, she reflected on the experience:
>
>> Everybody is going to suffer. We have no choice about that. But there is a choice we do have: to suffer alone or to suffer in the hands of a God who is all-powerful, and all-loving and whose hands are forever scarred by his own suffering.
>
> The "answer" to the problem of suffering is not a formula or an intellectual argument, but a relationship, a relationship with a God who is all-powerful, and all-loving, but who has suffered and does still suffer with his creatures.

JOSEPH TSON

In this modern era, there are many saints who have been chosen by God to suffer as Christ suffered. One such saint is Joseph Tson. In a series of messages on the subject "Union with Christ in Dangerous Times." Dr. Tson tells how having the right concept of a sovereign God helped him endure many months of KGB interrogation in Communist Romania. It began before he left England in order to go back to Romania. While in prayer, the Lord put a picture in his mind to illustrate the situation into which he was going. He saw a lone sheep surrounded by wolves and heard the Lord ask him, "Joseph, how much chance do you think this sheep has of surviving, let alone of converting the wolves?"

Pastor Tson replied, "Lord, you are my king. If you say, 'Go to the wolves,' I say, 'Yes, your majesty!' and I go to the wolves. But you are also my Father, and I have just learned that I have a Father who sends some of his children to the wolves. Help me to understand this."

Immediately, he heard the voice of Jesus say, "My Father sent me as a sheep among wolves. As my Father sent me, so I am sending you."

With this picture in mind, Joseph went back to Romania. Later, when he was arrested by the KGB, the Lord gave him another image. He was sitting by himself across the table from six powerful, notoriously evil men. But in his heart, Joseph saw strings attached to these men as the Lord moved them around like puppets. This comic portrait of his enemies as puppets on a string being manipulated by his God gave him peace and boldness in the presence of his interrogators. During those months of brutal treatment, something remarkable happened. Joseph's confidence in God's sovereign control gave him the freedom to show love to those who were persecuting him, and boldness in the face of their threats. Gradually, some of the wolves began to soften, and in the end, some even became sheep. Eventually, God brought Joseph safely to America and gave him a vital ministry preaching the gospel to Romania on Radio Free America.

Understanding that God is sovereign is a crucial kingdom perspective without which we will never be able to complete our journey. It is a perspective that requires faith. It requires trusting God's heart for us and trusting that He is in control even when He doesn't explain what He is doing. If we are going to develop intimacy with God and learn to walk with Him on a heart-focused journey, we have to learn to trust His sovereign hand.

The point of understanding God's sovereignty is not to be able to explain why we suffer or to know what the good is that God wants to accomplish or how God will overcome the evil in our lives. The point is hope. God wants us to know that we have hope because He is good and He is sovereign. As we learn to depend on that hope and trust God's plan for us and His heart toward us, we find peace.

FAITH

In his commentary on the opening chapters of Matthew, D. A. Carson tells the story about two Israelites having a conversation on the eve of the tenth plague. One has great faith; the other has weak faith. The one with weak faith says, "I'm worried. These plagues have been awful and this last one is supposed to be the worst of them all. I love my son. I don't want to see him die!" The one with great faith says, "Did you put the blood on the door frame of your house like Moses said?" "Yes," the man of weak faith answered, "but it doesn't feel like enough. There must be more that I can do to make sure my son is safe!" To which the man of great faith replied, "Well, I'm not worried. I'm going to get a good night's sleep. I put the blood on the door frames just as God asked, and I am confident my son will be safe." That night, when the angel of death passed through the Israelite camp, what do you think happened to the sons of these two men? Did the son of the man with weak faith die? Of course not! He had obeyed. He had put the blood on the doorposts.

The point is this: It does not require great faith to produce great miracles, because the power is not in the faith but in God—the object of our faith. What great faith produces is confidence. It is the ability to rest in the midst of the storm. Bill Gillham tells a story that illustrates this well. Imagine you are being chased by a bear. He is charging at you in a rage, but in the distance you see a log cabin. You have just enough of a head start to beat the bear to the cabin, slam the door in his face and lock the door. Now that you are in the cabin you are safe. The wood is thick, the lock is strong, and the bear is not getting in. If you have great faith in the cabin, you can relax, take a nap, eat some food and enjoy yourself. However, if you have weak faith, you could worry and fret about every possible thing that could go wrong. You could even work yourself into such a state of panic that you die of a heart attack in a room in which you are actually quite safe.

Christians with weak faith live with a distorted view of God's sovereignty and love. Their weak faith is the result of their faulty perspective of what God is really like. This is why one of the central practices of a heart-focused walk with God is meditation on those Scriptures and truths that help build a clear mental image of God as someone we trust.

THANKFULNESS

One of the ways we build a healthy view of God is by cultivating the habit of gratitude. In her classic book *The Hiding Place,* Corrie Ten Boom tells the gripping story of her arrest for hiding Jews from the Nazis during World War II. As punishment she was sentenced to hard labor in a concentration camp and was later moved to the infamous extermination camp of Ravensbruck. Miraculously, a clerical error led to her release just weeks before all women her age were executed. Corrie's story is a study in the sovereign work of God. Not only was her release a clear sign of God's work, she relates another story in her book about the time she learned to thank God in everything and not just when things were going well.

The barracks to which she and her sister Betsy were assigned was infested with fleas. On top of everything else they had to endure, this was just too much for Corrie. Couldn't God at least get rid of the fleas?!!! At Betsy's encouragement, Corrie agreed to give God thanks for the fleas, even if it was just an act of sheer obedience. Not long after that Betsy overheard some guards talking. It turned out they never inspected the barracks where Corrie and Betsy stayed. Why? Because of the fleas! Instantly, Corrie realized that God had put the fleas in her living quarters in order to give them privacy from the guards. This allowed them to conduct worship services every night and read from the Bible God had enabled her to smuggle into the camp. Seeing God's sovereign hand at work enabled Corrie to give thanks with true joy and not just trusting obedience.

Giving thanks in the midst of heartache and disappointment is perhaps the most fundamental way in which we acknowledge the sovereignty of God. It is a statement that we believe God is good regardless of the circumstances and that He has a plan that will bring us what is good.

SPIRITUAL EXERCISE

I Kings 6 tells the story of a man who had a dramatic perspective change that completely altered the way he looked at his circumstances. The city of Dothan was surrounded by a very visible, tangible enemy—an army from Syria. To all eyes it looked like Elisha was doomed to die. But he was unafraid. Why? He had a different perspective than everyone else. He saw that God was very much in control of the situation and that the real power was found in the unseen angelic army that had the unfortunate army from Syria surrounded.

1. In what areas of your life would it help to see the unseen world and know that God is actually in control of an area that seems completely out of control? How would it make you feel to know that God has an unseen army ready to fight on your behalf?

2. How has your view of God been impacted by this chapter?

3. How has your view of yourself and your circumstances been impacted by the lessons so far?

DISCUSSION STARTERS FOR SMALL GROUPS

1. How would you define sovereignty?

2. How is the idea of sovereignty comforting?

3. What ideas were stirred in your heart as you read this chapter?

4. Do you know a story of a time when God permitted, used, and over came evil?

5. Do you have an example of this from your own life?

6. How is the mental image of God as a divine chess player helpful to you?

6 PERSPECTIVE 3: SPIRITUAL WARFARE

BATTLE WITH THE WORLD

The last two chapters talked about two crucial perspectives that need to shape our mental picture of how life works, if we want to live with freedom and confidence as children of God. In the next two chapters, we are going to look at what our enemy the devil is doing to distort those pictures and make sure that our views of God, ourselves, and our world are as "messed up" as possible.

Perspective three is spiritual warfare. You cannot understand your life or the world in which you live until you realize that this planet is a battleground and that your life is lived in the context of a very real war. This is a war that can reduce you to a level of spiritual ineffectiveness in your life and witness for Christ and that can ultimately destroy you if you don't learn how to fight with confidence based on your position "in Christ" and His complete victory over our enemy (Colossians 2:15).

I have been aware of the reality of the war for a long time. When I was seven years old I saw a demon sitting in the next room staring at me. My parents were gone and my babysitter and my sister couldn't see it. I was the only one. It scared me so badly I started to scream. Nothing they could do calmed me down. Thankfully, the thing left as soon as my parents walked in the door. This happened more than once, and soon my parents took me to see a doctor. He said that I was having nightmares while I was awake. I thought he was crazy. I had never been more awake in my life! Eventually my parents taught me how to take authority over demons in the name of Jesus; and after I stood up to this intruder, it never came back.

There is a context to this story, some of which I only learned later in life. When my father was a missionary in Sierra Leone, West Africa, he saw things related to the occult and witchcraft that nothing in seminary or the church had prepared him to face. When he returned to the States and took a position teaching missions, he was determined to give other missionaries the training they needed to fight and win the war he knew they would face. News of his study and teaching about spiritual warfare spread, and one day a Christian counselor asked him to see a client that she had come to suspect was afflicted by demons. My father and mother agreed to meet with her, and over a period of time helped her come to freedom from her torment. It was shortly after this that I saw the demon in the dining room. Satan was trying to send a message to my parents: "Don't mess with me or I'll mess with your kids!" They got the message. The devil was offering them a deal: "Leave me alone and I'll leave you alone." It was a tempting proposition, but my parents were wise enough to know that you never make deals with the devil. This enemy is a liar by nature, and he will never keep his end of such a deal. He loves, however, to have Christians admit that they are afraid of him. He knows he is defeated. The tragedy is that all too often believers do not believe this at a level that leads to action. The Bible doesn't say, "Leave the devil alone and he will leave you alone." It says, "Resist the devil and he will flee from you."

Since that time my parents have helped hundreds of people find freedom in Christ. My father has taught on the subject for years, written two books on the subject, and worked with Neil Anderson and Freedom in Christ ministries for nearly two decades. Today, I am following in my parents' footsteps; counseling, teaching, and helping to awaken the church to the reality of the battle we face.

BATTLE BASICS

Several years ago, I was watching the movie *Hook* with my nieces and nephews when it occurred to me that this movie had done a remarkable job of capturing the essence of Satan's strategy in the battle for our hearts. In that movie Peter Pan has grown up, married, and come to have children of his own. Meanwhile, back in Neverland, Captain Hook dreamed of a final confrontation with his old nemesis. Hook's strategy in this conflict parallels Satan's strategy with us. He launched a plan to deceive Peter's children into believing lies about their father so that they would come to believe that Captain Hook loved them and their father did not. He actually conducted a class for the kids on the subject, "Why parents hate their children." The goal of his strategy was that on the day of battle, Peter's children would choose to fight *against* their father and *with* Captain Hook. In the same way, Satan uses a variety of tactics to deceive us into believing lies about God that keep us from intimacy with Him. Our adversary wants to rob God of His children so that on the day of battle God's children will actually choose to fight against their heavenly Father and for the kingdom of darkness.

Satan's primary weapon in this battle is deception. Satan cannot create his own reality. He cannot change the fact that God is good. He cannot change the fact that in Christ we are saints who "in Christ" are holy and blameless, or that we have been chosen in Christ for eternal blessing, or that we are members of God's family who are dearly loved and wonderfully secure in the palm of His hand. But what Satan can do is challenge our picture of this reality. This is what he did to Adam and Eve. He got them to doubt God's goodness and embrace a view of God that called into question the motives of His heart. Why did he do this? He did it because he knows that when God looks bad, sin looks good. The roaring lion wants to lure the sheep away from the shepherd where they will be easy prey. When you have a father you can't trust and who doesn't really love you, you will be open to lots of wrong ways to find the love and security we all need.

Satan needs to blind people to the truth about God and the truth about the battle in order to gain control over them and separate them from God.

If we knew the truth about God, we would desire Him passionately; so Satan has to use deception to make God look less attractive. Imagine what life would be like if an invisible person could follow you around and whisper in your ear deviant ideas about life. If you did not believe such a person existed, you would assume that all of those deviant thoughts were yours. This shadowy figure could exercise tremendous influence in your life. If you did not catch on to what was happening, that person could quite easily "take you captive to do his will" (2 Tim. 2:24).

This war for our hearts is fought on two fronts. There is a battle within and a battle without. The next chapter will look at the battle within and how the enemy uses wounds, lies, and issues from the past to separate us from God. This chapter will focus on the battle with the world and three of Satan's most common strategies to separate us from God. You can remember them with the word SIN: seduction, intimidation, and name-calling.

SEDUCTION

The devil's primary ally in this war is the world. The world can also be thought of as the devil's mistress. She is seductive and enticing, but ultimately deadly. She alternately flirts with us then rejects us, but keeps us hoping that we will find what we are looking for in the pleasure and power she has to offer. The world is personified by the Woman Folly in the book of Proverbs. She spouts a message that the good life is found in what she has to offer. She makes us feel that we are missing out on something exotic and wonderful and that we need a certain amount of sin in our lives in order to have fun. "Do whatever you please," she says. "Don't let anyone tell you how to live. God is no fun. He takes the fun out of life. If you want to have a good time, come be with me!"

The world captures our imagination with beauty, power, and the potential of freedom without accountability. It entices us to sin and blinds us to the fact that sin is spiritual adultery. It is cheating on the most beautiful and amazing person in the universe in order to be with the most despicable creature in the universe. James writes,

You adulterous people, don't you know that friendship with the world is hostility toward God? Anyone who chooses to be a friend of the world becomes an enemy of God (James 4:4).

In I John 2:15 we read,

Do not love the world or anything in the world. If anyone loves the world, love for the Father is not in them. For everything in the world—the lust of the flesh, the lust of the eyes, and the pride of life—comes not from the Father but from the world.

To love the world is to believe that the world can give you good things that God either can't or won't give to you. It is to view the world as the source of the good life you seek. This does not mean that the good things in life are evil. God delights in and often promises such things as wealth, joy, romance, our own land, and a good name. The problem is not in desiring these things but in looking to the world to supply them rather than to God. The lie is found in believing that the world is a more reliable provider than our heavenly Father. We see this in Hosea. The prophet Hosea was told to marry a prostitute. Can you imagine what a scandal it must have caused for a prophet of God to marry such a person, especially in that culture? Her name was Gomer. She bore him three children, but then something happened—a falling out, a seduction, a disenchantment with the routines of being a wife and mother—we don't know exactly what it was. But, whatever the reason, she left him and returned to her life of prostitution. There was money to be made and a life of luxury to be had for a successful prostitute. Listen to Gomer's words in Hosea 2:5, "I will go after my lovers, who give me my food and my water, my wool and my linen, my olive oil and my drink." She was like the Christian who thinks the world is the source of the good life they hope to find.

God's response to Gomer's betrayal provides an interesting study in the nature of God's heart. First, He cut her off from her lovers. "I will block her path with thorn bushes. I will wall her in so that she cannot find her way. She will chase after her lovers but not catch them" (2:6). This sounds a lot like the story of many people I know who have gone searching for the good life through the pursuit of worldly success, got a taste of it, then spent the rest of their lives addicted to the pursuit, like a user who has been given a taste of cocaine. God mercifully cut Gomer off from her lovers, though it must have been painful and traumatic at the time.

God did not stop there. He brought Gomer to ruin. "I will ruin her vines and her fig trees, which she said were her pay from her lovers; I will make them a thicket, and wild animals will devour them" (2:13). God had to bring Gomer to a place of total surrender. What Gomer didn't realize and what many of us often miss is that God was trying to rescue her. The path she was on was doomed to disaster. He simply brought a taste of that disaster to her doorstep while there was still time to repent.

Just when a skeptic might think that God was about to destroy Gomer once and for all, He does something unexpected. God makes an extraordinary announcement: "I am now going to woo her!" (Hosea 2:14). God had cut her off in order to bring her back to Himself and renew His love to her. In the end, we see that God's opposition to Gomer was intended not so much to punish her as to prepare her heart to receive His love. Gomer's condition had become so desperate that she was sold into slavery. In an extraordinary display of mercy, the Lord told Hosea to go to the slave market and buy her freedom. But God's kindness did not stop there. Hosea was to take Gomer back into his home and let her stay there for a set period of time, and then marry her once again!

The story of Gomer and Hosea is basically the Old Testament version of the prodigal son (Luke 15). It is a story of grace and God's provision for those who have been deceived by the world's seductions and led on a journey of shame and destruction. This is good news for each of us. For who of us has not been deceived into doing things of which we are utterly ashamed? Your life may be filled with the consequences of such foolish decisions, but it does not have to be the end of the story. It does not mean that God's love for you has ended. He still desires to enter into a sacred romance with you. But He is a jealous God. He is not willing to share you with the world. Repent. Cut yourself off from the love of the world. Turn to Him and He will take you as you are and begin to transform you into the person He always knew you could be.

INTIMIDATION

Satan likes to hide behind the world, but he doesn't like to hide forever. Sooner or later he wants to be known . . . and feared. Fear is a form of worship. This is why the phrase "the fear of the Lord" is often used in the Bible to describe worship. God wants us to have a proper fear of His wrath and recognize the devastation that a life of sin will inevitably bring. God wants us to fear Him in order to spare us the pain caused by folly. The devil wants us to fear him the way a slave fears the whip. God wants children who serve Him out of love. The devil wants slaves who serve him out of fear. Like the white witch in the Chronicles of Narnia, Satan is more than willing to dole out a few "sweeties" if that is what it takes to ensnare someone and make them captive to his will. But there is no "sweetness" in his heart.

One of the devil's intimidation tactics is to show us a display of power that leads us to believe the lie that his power can rival God's. We see this in many horror stories. There is often an unearthly being in these myths that cannot be destroyed. It is never truly defeated and thus creates the illusion of god-like immortality. The essence of horror is being locked in a reality too terrible to imagine with no hope of escape. Sadly, this is the way some people describe their lives. It is what leads many to attempt suicide, because they have come to believe they are locked in a horrible existence with no hope of real change.

One of the reasons Satan chooses to use displays of paranormal activity is that it confronts us with a power greater than our own. He wants to drive us to one of two extremes: either to embrace the power and seek to use it for our own purposes by practicing the occult or to run from the power and live in fear of it. Either way, he wins. God wants us to discover the power available to us in Christ and learn to stand against the schemes of the enemy in that strength.

Sadly, many people get ensnared in the occult because they are looking for wisdom or power to give them a sense of control. Satan often entices people with the "inside information" that he provides through mediums, spiritists, channelers, and fortune tellers who practice divination and astrology. I once saw an episode of "Oprah" in which an occultist was giving messages from deceased relatives to various members of the audience. People were crying and finding comfort from the news that every one of their relatives was doing well in heaven and didn't want them to be concerned about them. Such people do not contact the dead. They contact demons who knew the dead people and are able to give information about them and even imitate them. I had a friend whose sister was "mentally ill." Every Friday afternoon, she would begin to speak with her grandmother's voice and give orders to her father. Her condition only changed once the demon making this happen was challenged in the name of Jesus and evicted.

Satan also entices people with supernatural power that enables them to cast spells and curses or do other magical acts. This is the same type of occult power that was used by Pharaoh's magicians to turn their sticks into snakes and water into blood. It is a power that was common in ancient paganism and continues to be practiced in modern paganism and the New Age movement.

Unfortunately, many Christians have chosen the path of fear. I know Christians who don't even want to hear the word "demon." They treat the devil like a bee—hoping that if they leave him alone, he'll leave them alone. We are afraid that if we become knowledgeable about the war, we will have to fight and that if we remain in ignorance, we will be safe. But nothing could be further from the truth. Satan must jump up and down with joy at such thinking. There is a reason that Paul commanded us to put on the whole armor of God and be prepared to fight. The battle is real.

NAME CALLING

Satan is called the accuser of the brothers in Revelation 12:10. Not only does he tempt us through seduction and attack us through intimidation, he also accuses us through "name calling." When the Spirit convicts of sin, He is direct but gentle and shows us a path to repentance. When Satan accuses, he attacks us at the core of who we are. He labels us with our sin and attempts to get us to receive that label as our true identity.

You can often recognize the voice of the adversary by the name calling he does—"idiot, pervert, loser"—and by the personal nature of the attack—"You call yourself a Christian? A person like you has no business being in ministry. There is something fundamentally wrong with you!"

Rich Miller, the president of Freedom in Christ ministry, tells a story about a missionary in Mexico who drove a powder blue minivan that seemed to scream "American!" There were some corrupt police in that town running a scam. At an intersection with a light stuck on red in all four directions one officer waved the powder blue van through the light only to have another officer pull it over (obviously hoping for a bribe) and give the driver a ticket for running a red light! Upset about the situation, the missionaries went to see a friend of theirs who was a high ranking official in the government. He gave them his card and said, "If you have any problems with the police again, show them my card and tell them to take it up with me."

Well, it didn't take long until they got pulled over again. This time, however, they rolled down their window, and flashed the card to the policeman. They watched his face turn pale as he recognized the name on the card. Straightening up, the officer informed them that there had been a misunderstanding and they were free to go.

It is important for us to understand that not every thought that comes into our head is ours. Some come from the Holy Spirit and some come from the devil. One way to tell the difference is that Satan seeks to separate us from God through accusation; the Spirit shows the path to relationship. So, one test we can use to distinguish which thoughts are from God and which are from the devil is to ask, "Does this thought prompt me toward intimacy with God or away from it?" Another test is to ask whether the thought breeds fear or faith. If the thought brings sorrow, ask, "If I follow where this sorrow is leading will I draw closer to God, or move farther from Him?"

The Scripture tells us to take every thought captive and make it obedient unto Christ (2 Corinthians 10:5). Satan often traps us in false guilt over things that have been forgiven long ago or over things that are not even sins. Other times, the devil tempts us, saying, "Go through that red light, everyone does it." Then as soon as we do, he accuses us, "You horrible person! I can't believe you did that again!" At times like these, God wants us to confess our sin and reconnect with Him. He wants to walk through our failure with us. But the enemy's accusations often take our minds captive and separate us from God needlessly. At times like these, Jesus wants us to flash his business card and tell Satan to take his accusations to our Lord and deal with Him!

WINNING THE BATTLE FOR YOUR MIND

A key weapon in our battle with the world is the authority that is ours in Christ. There are two opposite extremes Christians often embrace related to authority. The first is to believe that we have no authority over demons. This view is usually based on the passage in Jude in which Michael did not dare to rebuke the devil, but said, "The Lord rebuke you." This sounds reasonable until you realize that Michael and Lucifer were peers. They were both angels. Also, the context of Jude is dealing with false prophets who are not Christians and thus do not have authority. The basis of our authority in Christ is rooted in the idea that we have been raised with Christ and *seated* with Him in heaven at God's right hand far above angelic principalities and powers. We have thus been given a position of authority and the right to speak, act, and pray in the name of Jesus. Some however take this to another extreme by suggesting that when we speak in the name of Jesus, it is as if Jesus Himself is speaking and that, if we have enough faith, we can speak reality into existence just as Jesus can. However, if this were true, we could just cast Satan into hell and be done with it. But that is not within the scope of our authority. You see, our authority is limited by law in the same way that a referee or a police officer has authority that is limited by law. A referee can take the ball away from one team and give it to another if he thinks a player has broken one of the rules. But the referee cannot eject someone from the game because he has bad breath! Bad breath may be offensive, but it is not against the rules. In the same way, our authority as Christians is limited by divine law. We can use it to enforce God's will, but not our own.

There are four principles (R. E. S. T.) that help me remember how to use the authority that is ours in Christ in the battle with the world.

R. RECOGNIZE THE ENEMY. Remind yourself that not every thought that enters your head is yours. When I get into a bad place emotionally, my wife frequently asks me, "Honey, where is that thought coming from?" Thoughts are like the cars of a train. It is easier to stop the train before it gains momentum. The more box cars you let go by, the harder it is going to be to stop the train. In the same way, the sooner you recognize that the engineer of the train of thought that is heading your way is the devil, the sooner you can resist him. If you let too many enemy thoughts go by, it can become almost impossible to keep from sin.

E. EXPOSE THE ENEMY. Once you recognize that the thought in your head is from the enemy, you need to expose him. There have been times of attack, when I have literally caught myself saying, "Gotcha! Now get out of here!" One of the first times this happened, I was simply walking across a parking lot at the school where I taught but was wrestling with anxious thoughts. Suddenly it occurred to me that it was not God sending me anxious thoughts, and I certainly wasn't trying to think anxious thoughts. At that point a light went on in my head: "This must be the enemy." As soon as I exposed the problem as an attack of the enemy, it left. Sometimes just exposing the fact that an attack is coming from the enemy and not just from your flesh is enough to defeat it.

S. STAND AGAINST THE ENEMY. As the story of the missionary and the business card suggests, there comes a time when we need to stand up to the devil and use our authority to make him leave. James tells us to resist the devil and he will flee (5:7). According to Ephesians 6:11, the very reason we have been given the armor of God is to stand against the devil's schemes. We do this by first submitting ourselves to God through confession and obedience, and then commanding the devil to flee in the name of Jesus. Luther is credited with saying, "You can't keep a bird from landing on your head, but you can keep it from building a nest there." The sooner we recognize enemy thoughts, expose them, and stand against him, the less chance he will have of building a nest.

T. TURN TO THE TRUTH. It is important to replace the lie of the enemy with God's truth. Ask the Spirit to show you the truth on which to take your stand. Jim Logan calls this "building a tower of truth." I learned the importance of this early in life. I remember one day in elementary school that I was in my room battling with negative thoughts. I kept telling myself, "Stop thinking about that; resist, fight!" But the more I focused on the fight, the worse it got. Finally the Spirit prompted me that it wasn't enough to resist, I had to replace the negative thoughts with the truth. Philippians 4:8 came to mind about setting your mind on things that are good and excellent. It was as I began to focus on truth that I experienced a clear victory over the negative emotions that had been plaguing me.

SPIRITUAL EXERCISES

My father tells the story of a theology professor who was invited to speak at a church in Africa several years ago. While he was speaking a woman levitated out of her seat, floated to the aisle and began speaking in an unknown language. Several of the church elders gathered around her, dealt with the demon, then motioned for the speaker to continue. Recalling that experience the professor said, "Somewhere between the time that lady rose out of her seat and came down in the aisle, my theology changed!"

The Bible is filled with accounts of the reality of the battle we face and warns us to resist the devil and put on the armor of God. If we want to live a victorious Christian life, we must live with a warfare perspective.

1. Pay attention to the battle for your mind this week. Look for opportunities to recognize, expose, and stand against the enemy. You might even want to make yourself a business card to keep with you in order to remind yourself of the need to use your authority in Christ to make the enemy flee. Take time to write in your journal about your experience in this area.

2. Reflect on the enemy's tactics in your life. Take time to answer the following questions.

a. What names does the enemy call you?

64

b.   What names does the Spirit of Truth call you?

c.   Have you ever been intimidated by the enemy? What did you do about it? How would you handle it, today?

d.   In what areas has the world's seduction been most effective in your life?

3.   Memorize John 10:10, "A thief comes only to steal, kill, and destroy. I have come that they may have life and have it in abundance." God's goal for you is an abundant life. The devil wants to rob you of that life. As you journal this week ask the Lord some of these questions.

DISCUSSION STARTERS FOR SMALL GROUPS

1.   Share with the group an insight from your journaling this week.

2.   How have you experienced spiritual warfare in your life?

3.   What examples of the world's seductive power have you seen?

4.   What examples of Satan's intimidation have you seen?

5.   What examples of Satan's accusational name calling have you experienced?

6.   How can understanding spiritual warfare help you walk more intimately with God?

7.   What insight from this chapter was most helpful to you?

7 PERSPECTIVE 3 (CONT.): SPIRITUAL WARFARE

BATTLE WITHIN

In chapter two, I wrote that Jim Wilder defines maturity as your ability to act like yourself. Let that sink in for a moment. Many define themselves by their failures or weaknesses as if they are acting most like themselves when they are depressed or angry or failing. Others define themselves by the roles they play and the masks they wear. But in reality these are the things that are keeping us from acting like ourselves. Most of the people I know live with emotional baggage that keeps them from acting like themselves. If someone "pushes their buttons" they resort to childish behavior like pouting or throwing a tantrum. When it happens to me, I often become defensive and very immature. One of the reasons so many of us struggle with this is that we have gotten stuck in our personal and emotional development. There are certain skills and types of knowledge that need to be mastered in order to function as a mature adult. When trauma interrupts that process, it can lead to immaturity that results in some very serious consequences that bring destruction into our lives rather than life.

Emotions are an important part of life, but they can be hard to understand. A tool we can call the ABC'S of emotions provides a framework for dealing with our emotions and the emotions of others.

A. ALARM SYSTEM. Emotions are the alarm system of the soul. Just as your body has the ability to feel, so your soul has the ability to feel. Your body's ability to feel pain is a warning system to protect you from serious damage. People who cannot feel physical pain often burn themselves and damage themselves in other ways because they have no sensation warning them of the harm they are doing to their bodies. In a similar way, emotions are a warning system that something is going on in your heart that needs your attention. If it doesn't get addressed, it can often do great harm.

B. BUTTONS[2]. We all go through life wearing emotional vests that are covered with buttons. Each of these buttons is linked to a powder keg of emotion deep inside, so that when one of them is pushed, the powder keg explodes. Sometimes the emotion is anger. Sometimes it is depression; sometimes fear or shame. Whatever the emotion, we cannot help but feel it when our buttons get pushed because our brains have been programmed to respond that way. Instead of dealing with our buttons and the powder keg of emotion inside, most of us learn how to dance our way through life in such a way that our buttons rarely get pushed. If we get good enough at the dance, we can begin to believe that we have no issues, because they rarely get triggered.

C. CHOICES. We cannot keep ourselves from feeling emotions any more than we can keep our toes from hurting when we stub them on the leg of a table. However, we can control the choices we make on how we respond to our emotions. On the journey to maturity, it is important to recognize when our buttons are getting pushed. One clue is that we overreact emotionally. For example, if my wife uses a certain tone of voice when she talks to me and something inside of me wants to smash in a wall with a baseball bat, that's overreacting. Even if I choose to control myself, the fact that the emotion is so strong tells me it's time to "look under the hood." It's acting like the immature boy rather than the mature self—the real person God designed me to be. It is certainly not acting like myself

---

2. Many of the ideas shared here were inspired by the teaching of Ed Smith and Theophostic Ministry.

to respond in that way. It is not what people would expect from me. So, when I experience an extreme emotion, I need to choose to handle it in a mature manner. I also need to get away and talk to God about it and find out why that emotion is so strong. At times like that, it is important to ask God to take you to the source of your problem.

S. SOURCE. The powder keg of emotion within us that is triggered when people push our buttons is not born there. It is not our nature. You cannot say, "That's just the way I am." It is a learned flesh response to the experiences of our past. Perhaps hearing my wife's tone of voice reminds me subconsciously of that tone being used in an unjust way when I was a child and the lies Satan told me about that experience. It means something to me that evokes strong emotion. When present events generate feelings and beliefs similar to those from our past, we tap into a reservoir of emotion created when we were young, which is why we tend to revert to childish behavior when those buttons are pushed. If you ask God to take you to the source, He will probably lead you to a time in your formative years when you experienced that same intense emotion—a time when Satan's lie took root in your heart. Ask the Lord to expose the lie and show you the truth.

A few years ago, I met with a man in his late thirties who was stuck in an addiction to pornography. He had been to several counselors and programs, but always returned to his addiction. It became clear in listening to him that no one had dealt with the source of his problem. They were hoping that confession and accountability would take care of it. The reality was that two formative events in his past were driving his addiction. First, he had an older brother who was very athletic and popular. He was big and strong while this man was a "late bloomer" who went through high school with an underdeveloped body. By comparison the boy felt inferior to his brother and the lie took root that he wasn't a real man. What was ironic about this was that when he walked into my office I remember being impressed with the way he looked and literally had the thought, "Now this is a man's man."

The other formative event at the root of his addiction happened when he was a young teen. He was at a beach on an outing with some friends and slipped away by himself into the woods. While he was there, he was jumped by some older teens and sexually assaulted. In the midst of this trauma two lies took root in his heart. First was the lie that God had abandoned him. Second was the belief that this would not have happened to him if he was a real man. In the midst of the intense emotions he was feeling, he prayed and asked the Lord to enter this memory and heal the pain caused by that event.[3] I listened as he described a beam of light that came from the sky and began to wash him in a warm light. The picture of his abusers began to fade away and he found himself alone in the presence of God. Tears began to flow and I asked, "How true does it feel that God has abandoned you?" "Not true at all," he responded. We talked for a while and then he asked God to reveal how He saw him. He closed his eyes and began to pray. As I waited for his response, a smile began to cross his face and he said, "I see myself dressed like a cowboy." "What does that mean to you?" I asked. He looked at me and said, "It means I'm a real man."

The trauma in his life had created fertile ground for the devil's lies that caused him to get stuck on his maturity journey. As a result, he was not free to act like himself. He had turned to pornography to feel like a man and left feeling like a fraud. Habits and addictions like pornography always have a source and they often cannot be fully overcome until that source is identified and healed.

WOUNDS, LIES, AND VOWS

It is impossible to live in this fallen world without getting wounded in the battle. These wounds often create precisely the opportunity Satan is looking for to plant his lies in our hearts. If we believe his lies, we begin to make vows about how we will live our lives as if those lies are true. These vows will shape the way we live and create patterns that will control the direction of our lives. I learned a simple pattern from John Eldredge's teaching that has

Wounds create broken hearts.

---

3. It was David Seaman's book *Healing for Damaged Emotions* that first introduced my family and me to the idea of healing prayer and inviting Jesus to visit people at the point of their pain and bring healing.

helped me explain the process by which strongholds develop in our lives. I call it WLVS: the demonic radio network. WLVS stands for wounds, lies, vows, and strongholds. It describes a common process that demons use to build strongholds in our lives.

1. WOUNDS. There are basically two types of heart wounds: Type A and Type B. Type A trauma is caused by the absence of good things that we need. Type B trauma is caused by the bad things that happen to us—abuse of all kinds. A type trauma occurs when you live with a father who never says, "I love you," or who neglects to prepare you for life or protect you from evil. It occurs when your mother is so preoccupied with her own pain that she isn't there for you when you go through yours. Type B trauma occurs when you are wounded by cruel words or deeds. Both types of abuse break our hearts leaving a gap that is wide open to receiving Satan's lies.

2. LIES. Lies are like seeds. When they are planted in the heart, they grow into vines that produce all kinds of bad fruit—negative emotions, addictive behaviors, and sinful choices. What we believe creates a foundation from which we live life. Several years ago, I heard Tony Campolo deliver a speech at a seminary chapel in which he said, "It is not the events of the past that mold us into what we are. It is what those events *mean* to us that molds us into what we are. My mother dies; your mother dies. I go into a depression; you don't. Why? Because what your mother dying *means* to you is different

Wounds create broken hearts.

than what my mother dying *means* to me." He is right. I see this all the time. When my heart is wounded, Satan plants a lie in the broken place of my heart that interprets the event. His lies have two main targets: my view of God and my view of myself. They teach me that I cannot trust God or that I am a flawed, unlovable person. If our hearts embrace those lies, they become the foundation for the vows we make about how we will live life.

3. VOWS. Vows are those deep convictions we develop about how

we will live life. They usually begin with the words, "I will **always**_____"
or "I will never _____." For example, "I will never trust anyone again!"
Or, "I will prove everyone wrong." Such vows create our identity. They
form our personality and often become the masks behind which we hide.

I once heard John Trent tell a story that illustrates how wounds and
lies lead to vows that mold our lives. It went something like this. There
was a family with three boys who
had an alcoholic father. When he got
drunk, he would get violent and un-
predictable. One night he came home
intoxicated and began to hit his wife.
The oldest son stepped in, shoved his
dad out of the way, and swore he'd kill
him if he ever hit his mom again. Then
he stormed out of the house in a rage
and slammed the door behind him.
The middle son wasn't big enough to
bully his dad; so he became a pleaser.
"Can I get you anything, dad? Do you

The Seed of Satan's lie grow
into the vine of our vows.

want your paper? Your slippers? Another drink?" The youngest son was
too little to understand what was happening. He went and hid under the
bed until it was over.

Can you see how this event and others like it molded the vows these
boys made about the way they would handle life? The eldest fought his
way through life and vowed that he would never let anyone hurt him or
his loved ones again. The middle boy spent his life as a people-pleaser.
He vowed that he would never live with chaos again and would always
find a way to keep people happy. The youngest boy spent his life avoiding
hard things or running away from them. He vowed never to allow himself to be put into a troubling situation again. So he spent his life quitting
and running. My dad calls these responses: fighting, fixing, and fleeing.

STRONGHOLDS

Our vows are like vines that grow from the seed of Satan's lies. They produce the fruit of negative emotions and foolish behavior that we call stronglholds. Often, we go to coun- selors to deal with an addiction or a chronic emotional problem and do lit- tle more than "pick fruit." The time is spent finding ways to modify behavior or talk about past issues without tak- ing them to Christ. Until we get to the root causes of our issues, the vine will continue to grow and bear unwanted fruit. I call this the counterfeit John 15 experience. Instead of abiding in Christ and his word abiding in me so that I bear fruit for the kingdom, the enemy's word abides in me bearing fruit for his kingdom.

The vine of our vows bears the fruit of bondage to demonic strongholds.

A stronghold can be thought of as an area in our thinking that has come under the devil's control. It is characterized by a sense of hope- lessness that any real change is possible. 2 Corinthians 10:4-5 describes a stronghold with terms related to the mind. It describes a stronghold as ar- guments and high things that oppose the knowledge of God. It also gives us the good news that the Christian has spiritual weapons for demolishing the strongholds in our minds that enable us to "take every thought captive and make it obedient to Christ."

Dealing with the wounds in our hearts is not always a simple pro- cess, but there are some relatively straightforward things we can do to tear down the devil's strongholds. Here is a four-step process for dealing with strongholds that can be remembered with the word F. R. E. E. – Forgive, Repent, Eliminate, and Evict.

FORGIVE. To forgive someone is to cancel a debt. The Greek word *apoluso* means "to free from" or "to loose from." When we forgive, we release a person from the debt they owe to us. We also release them from the chains that keep us bound to them and to the power of sin. When we cancel a debt in this way, we release the other person from what is owed to us, but not from what is owed to God. In a sense, we are handing them over to God's collection agency and letting Him deal with the debt.

In this sense, forgiveness is a business transaction; not an emotion. However, to forgive someone from your heart requires getting in touch with your emotions. One of the ways to do this is to ask the Holy Spirit to bring to mind people we need to forgive and to help us remember them in a way that stirs our emotions. This is important because I have seen many people go through the motions of forgiveness without getting in touch with their heart, and it does them no good. On the other hand, I have seen people experience tremendous release by allowing themselves to get in touch with their pain and choosing to forgive from the heart as an act of obedience to their Lord.

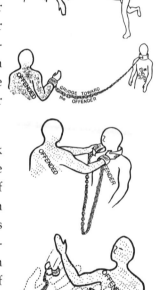

Forgiveness is a gift God gives us to unlock the chains of bitterness that keep us in bondage to the power of sin. Bitterness is the result of being sinned against or at least the perception that we have been sinned against. The images on this page were developed by an organization called Victorious Christian Living based in Phoenix, Arizona. It illustrates the process of forgiveness. An offender wounds you, creating a hurt with which you must now live. Forgiveness requires you to live with the consequences of another person's sin. The reality is that you have no choice but to live with these consequences. According to Neil Anderson, "The only choice [one has] is whether to do so in the bondage of bitterness or in the freedom of forgiveness"

As a result of the offense, you are now linked to the other person with a chain of bitterness. For the rest of your life, you will be connected to this person as long as you are bound to them by bitterness. You can move to another country or the other person could even die, but you will still be chained to them. The good news is that God has given you a gift. You can choose to cancel the debt and set yourself free. The process concludes by handing the chains of bitterness over to God.

After leading a person to forgive someone in this way, it is appropriate to encourage them to pray a blessing on the one who wronged them. For people who have truly forgiven, this is usually not hard to do. They want God to heal the hurts that drove the offending person to do evil. It also helps to confirm the reality of their decision to forgive and make it tangible.

I recently spoke at an Ethiopian church in the Washington D. C. area where a leader in the church shared his story of coming to freedom by choosing to forgive a group of soldiers who had beaten him and left him crippled in one foot, even though he had done nothing to provoke them. This man had made a vow in his heart to seek vengeance one day, but after becoming a Christian and then a leader in his church, he realized that he had to release these soldiers from his vow of vengeance and choose to forgive. This simple step had profound implications in the spirit realm. Sin lost its grip on him and peace flooded his heart. Compassion began to replace bitterness. He was free.

REPENT

The Greek word for repentance is *metanoia*, which means to change (*meta*) your mind (*noia*). The idea of repentance is not a grudging alteration of behavior. It is a transformation of how you think about your behavior so that you come to despise what you used to desire. The classic example of repentance in the Bible is the prodigal son. He began his journey in love with the world, believing firmly that the good life could be found on the path of rebellion. His repentance began when his eyes were opened and he saw his life in a whole new light. It was the transformation of belief that led to a transformation of behavior.

Someone once called repentance the happiest word in the English language. That struck me as odd because I was used to associating repentance with shame. But the more I thought about it, the more it made sense. Repentance means you get another chance. It is the promise of a new beginning and a fresh start.

Genuine repentance is different than mere confession. A person can confess to something without really wanting to change. Some signs that this is happening include the following

S. Seeking secrecy more than change. When a person has greater fear that people will learn of their failing than they do of gaining victory over sin, one must wonder about the sincerity of the repentance.

T. Trivializing the sin. Some people admit to a sin, but then dismiss it as "not that bad." Such trivialization of sin calls into question whether a real "change of mind" has occurred.

R. Resisting help. A person can admit to a failing, but resist help in dealing with the issues that led to the failure. This is often a sign of pride.

I. Introspection that leads to immobilization. Sometimes people dwell on their sin to such an extent that they virtually define their existence by their sin. They know they are "bad." They dwell on their "badness." They wallow in it as if they are victims and can develop a "poor me" attitude that sounds humble, but actually keeps the person from dealing with the problem.

P. Passing the blame to others. This one is as old as Adam: "I know I did it, but it wasn't my fault. If that person had done their part, I would not have sinned."

E. Excusing the sin. We humans have a tremendous capacity for self-deception. As long as there is an excuse for our behavior, we eliminate any expectation for change.

ELIMINATE. When kings led Israel in a revival, the first thing they did was to eliminate those objects that kept the people tied to idolatry. Under Hezekiah Israel "broke up the sacred pillars, chopped down the Asherah poles and tore down the high places and altars" (2 Chronicles 31:1). When Josiah led Judah to break from the paganism of Manasseh and return to the worship of Yahweh, we read that "he began to cleanse

Judah and Jerusalem of the high places, the Asherah poles, the carved images, and the cast images" (2 Chronicles 34:3). He went so far as to dig up the bones of the pagan priests and burn them on the altars they had used to worship Baal and Asherah (2 Chronicles 34:5).

In the New Testament, Paul led the Christians of Ephesus in the destruction of their occult paraphernalia. "Those who had practiced magic collected their books and burned them in front of everyone. So they calculated their value and found it to be 50,000 pieces of silver" (Acts 19:19). There is no fellowship between Christ and Satan (2 Corinthians 6:14-16), and there is a reason why Moses commanded Israel to destroy objects that had been used for pagan purposes (Deuteronomy 7:25-26). It is crucial that Christians destroy occult books and objects. (Don't sell them and pass on the problem!).

After watching her husband help a man in the church come to victory over several issues in his life by going through Neil Anderson's "Steps to Freedom," a pastor's wife asked her husband to take her through the steps. It happened to be about midnight on the Saturday before he was supposed to preach. Nevertheless, they dove into it. At one point the woman realized that she had some videos in her library that taught occult principles. She decided that the right thing to do was to destroy them. So, she got a trash bag and began throwing her entire collection of this popular television series into the trash, even though not all of them were oriented toward the occult. As she was doing this, a couple of the tapes stuck to the bottom of the drawer. She could not get them out no matter what she did. She asked her husband to help thinking he might have more strength. But the videos were being held in place by a spiritual force. It was not until she proclaimed, "in the name of Jesus I will throw these away," that they almost flew out of the drawer. That night was a turning point in her walk with the Lord. They finally finished around five in the morning, got a few hours of sleep, and went to church. Instead of preaching, the pastor asked his wife and the man he had taken through the steps to share their stories. The impact was powerful. In the pastor's own words, "You have to understand, the people of the church tolerate me; but they love my wife." When they heard this woman they respected so much tell of her need for freedom and how God had worked during the night, there wasn't a dry eye in the place.

EVICT. James 4:7 says, "Submit yourselves therefore to God, resist the devil and he will flee from you." We submit ourselves to God by obeying Him and through the practice of forgiveness, repentance, and the elimination of that which keeps us in bondage to the enemy. Once we have submitted to God in this way, we are in a position to resist the devil. Sometimes we resist the devil by taking our thoughts captive as I described in the last chapter (recognizing the enemy, exposing the enemy, standing against the enemy, and turning to the truth). There are times, however, when we resist the devil in tearing down strongholds.

There was a time in my life when I endured panic attacks every day for more than a week. Every day at five in the afternoon I could feel the sensation of fear rising through my body and settling over me for the night. Although I recognized it as an attack of the enemy and repeatedly commanded it to leave in the name of Jesus, it had no effect. I felt helpless and embarrassed that I couldn't gain victory over the fear. Eventually as I was talking with a friend about the problem, the root issue came to the surface. I was in a counseling situation at the time with someone who claimed to be interested in leaving an occult group. I was in over my head and I knew it. As I talked, the Lord led me to identify my core fear: I was afraid that I could not trust God to protect my family from the Satanists. As soon as I verbalized this belief and acknowledged it as a lie, something broke, and I was able to command the spirit of fear to leave. Once I did, I was able to evict the spirit in Jesus' name and the panic attacks stopped.

I do not tell the story to imply that all panic attacks are demonic or that they can all be fixed using a simple method. I share my story to demonstrate the fact that there are times when we need to remove legal ground and evict the tormentors that harass us, if we want to live in freedom.

Some people question whether it is necessary to deal with the past. Shouldn't we simply "forget the past" and "press on?" In response, I would simply point out that while the wounds may be in the past, the lies, vows, and strongholds are very much in the present. So is the powder keg of emotion and so are the buttons that keep getting pushed. The most effective way to deal with the past and move forward is to get to the root of our present issues. I would also point out that forgiveness and repentance, by their very nature, require dealing with the past; and I have never heard anyone suggest that these are unbiblical. Having said this, I recognize that some people live in the past. Their preoccupation with their wounds actually promotes dysfunction. Our goal should be to help people identify and overcome the obstacles to a deeper walk with God that are rooted in the past.

Obviously, reading one chapter on how to deal with the wounds of the past and going through a few exercises is not going to fix every problem in your life. The point of this chapter is not to provide a quick fix for all of your issues, but to point you in a direction that offers hope. I would encourage you to go through the process of forgiving, repenting, eliminating, and evicting. I would also encourage you to be aware of the lies and vows in your life that perpetuate the power of events from your past. Part of growing in intimacy with God is working through your issues with Him and taking time to talk to him about the "buttons" and the wounds, lies, and vows that fuel the powder keg within. Such a conversational, healing journey may be precisely the path God wants to use to lead you into a deeper walk with Him.

SPIRITUAL EXERCISE

The story of Zaccheus illustrates the life changing power of a new perspective. Zaccheus looked to the world for the good life he craved, and he became rich just as he hoped. But the world's wealth did not satisfy. Meeting with Jesus led to a change in perspective that led to a change in behavior. Is there a change in behavior that needs to happen in your life? Is there a stronghold from which you need to be set free? Ask the Lord to show you if there is an area in which He wants to work, then walk through some of the following exercises.

1. Ask God to bring to your mind any sin in your life that has you in bondage. Confess the sin, i.e., agree with God that it really is sin. Renounce your involvement with it and, by faith, receive God's forgiveness. Then ask God what steps He wants you to take to eliminate it from your life. Write those steps in a journal and share them with a friend.

2. Ask God to bring to mind any people you have wronged and show you what He wants you to do about that.

3. Ask God to bring to your mind any people you need to forgive. Allow yourself to feel the sting of what they did to you or of the good they withheld from you. Choose to forgive them as an act of obedience and ask God to show you what He wants you to know about that person or that situation.

4. Ask God to reveal an area of bondage in your life He wants to break. Ask Him what the first step is He wants you to take in overcoming that bondage. You may want to go through a specific bondage breaking prayer like those found at the Deeper Walk International website.

5. Go on a three-day fast. Eat no food and drink only water or pure juice. No sugar. No additives. You may feel sick at first, but notice how much your tastes change when you are done.

6. Embark on a 28 day journey to reform one habit in your life.

7. Celebrate your victories with some understanding friends. Enjoy a celebratory meal. Give gifts. Write notes. Find a way to share the joy.

Many of these steps can be done on your own, but it is often a good idea to meet with someone you trust. A very helpful way to jumpstart this process is to find a mature Christian (preferably older and of the same gender as you) and go through *The Steps to Freedom in Christ* developed by Neil Anderson.

DISCUSSION STARTERS FOR SMALL GROUPS

1. How did the idea of emotional buttons help you understand yourself better?

2. How important do you think it is to deal with buttons and strong holds? Why?

3. Do you have a story related to the issues raised in this chapter?

4. What insight from this chapter had the biggest impact on you?

5. Did you do any of the exercises? What impact did it have for you?

CONCLUSION

Heart focused discipleship begins with three core perspectives. (1) God loves you and wants you to experience a sacred romance with Him in which He speaks to your heart and walks through life with you. (2) The God who loves you is the sovereign Lord of the universe who is working all things together for your good and wants you to trust Him. (3) We have an enemy who uses seduction, intimidation and name calling to teach you lies about God and yourself in order to separate you from God and rob you of the sacred romance you were born to enjoy. If we want to live victorious Christian lives, we must fully embrace these three core perspectives.

In the next section of this book, we will explore four core practices that are fundamental to developing intimacy with God as we learn to move forward in this journey of the heart.

8 PRACTICE 1: SEEKING GOD

I recently learned what it means to be a dry drunk. A friend of mine who has led a number of Alcoholics Anonymous groups defines a dry drunk as someone who has quit drinking, but still craves alcohol. Though they force themselves to say "No," they constantly wish they could have a drink. For such people it is usually just a matter of time until they "fall off the wagon." I think I know what that must be like. I just finished a two week diet with no sugar, no caffeine, no dairy, no meat, and no wheat. I basically lived on vegetables, oats, fish, rice, and green tea! I tolerated the diet; in fact, my wife was amazed at how disciplined I was. But every day, I wished I could be eating something else. I counted down the days until I could eat "normally." Although I was able to discipline myself for a short period of time, I didn't really want to change my lifestyle. This is a problem many of us face as we seek to live in a manner "worthy of the Lord." It is one thing to read about a new way of thinking or to gain a new insight about living and agree that it would be good to live that way. It is quite another to make lifestyle changes that actually lead in a new direction.

A friend of mine recently invited me to attend a Dale Carnegie course on management. It was a very good course with lots of helpful information. But what set the event apart from other management training I have received is their commitment to coaching people as they practice what they have learned. They know that practicing what you learn is crucial to learning new skills, and that coaching helps make sure that you are practicing correctly. A phrase you hear a lot in Carnegie circles is that "practice doesn't make perfect; practice makes *permanent.*" Isn't that true? I can practice my golf swing all day, but if I am practicing a really bad golf swing, I am simply making that bad swing permanent. This highlights an important problem that many of us face. Our minds have been trained by the flesh to think incorrectly about life. If we are really going to change the way we live, we have to change the way we believe. As my father often says, "People may not live what they say they believe, but they will always live what they really believe." To change what we believe will require us to develop practices that reinforce new ways of thinking.

LEGALISM

As soon as you start talking about doing things to grow in your walk with God, fears can creep in that you are moving towards legalism. So, let's take a moment right now to address that issue.

The word legalism is related to law. You can see it in the word itself: legal-ism. Paul referred to it as being "under law." The term refers to the belief that your relationship with God is based on Law, i.e., on your performance rather than on faith in what God has done for you. It is not simply that you are trying to gain salvation by obedience to the Law; you are trying to earn the right to intimacy by your behavior. Under legalism when you obey, you are accepted; but when you disobey, you are rejected and unwelcome in God's presence until you repent. When a person's relationship with God is governed by Law, it tends to lead to extremes. On the one side are those who live in fear that they have not done enough to please God and earn His acceptance; so their shame keeps them from seeking intimacy with the Father. On the other side are those who live in pride (like the Pharisees) believing that they have performed well and earned God's blessing. Such people often develop extensive checklists of what constitutes sin and what is merely a "weakness" so that they can know exactly where they stand and how they compare to others.

Some people who reject legalism turn to "license." They reject all authority and anyone's right to impose rules on them. But the New Testament is filled with rules and commands us to submit to authority. The cure for legalism is not license, but grace; and the motive for obedience is not law, but love.

GRACE AND GOOD WORKS

The book of Titus contains one of the more politically incorrect verses in the Bible. Paul warns a young pastor on the island of Crete about the locals: "Even one of their own prophets has said, 'Cretans are always liars, evil brutes, lazy gluttons'" (1:12). As if that wasn't bad enough, check out the next verse, "This testimony is true!" (1:13). After reading this passage, my mind went to a video by George Otis called "Transformations." In it, he tells the story of a town in El Salvador that fit the description of first century Crete pretty well. It was a small town, but it had four jails and had to bus the extra scoundrels out of the city to jails in the next town when the four they had got full—which was pretty much every weekend. Alcoholism was epidemic, as was wife-abuse, sloth, witchcraft, idolatry, and poverty. But something happened in that city that changed everything. The city was transformed by the power of prayer and the courage and unity of the local Christians. Today, nearly 90% of the people in the town are believers. The jails have closed. The idolatry and witchcraft have gone. Marriages are staying together, and the economy has boomed.

The Crete of Paul's day was in need of this type of transformation, and the church was in need of leaders who broke the mold of Cretan culture by being "hospitable, lovers of what is good, who are self-controlled, upright, holy and disciplined." It is not surprising; therefore, that Paul uses the term "self-controlled" five times in fourteen verses. He urges Timothy to find elders who are self-controlled (1:8), to teach older men to be self-controlled (2:2), to train younger women to be self-controlled (2:5), and to encourage young men to be self-controlled (2:6). Finally, in 2:11-14 he explains the key to becoming self-controlled.

> For the grace of God that brings salvation has appeared to all men. It teaches us to say, "No" to ungodliness and worldly passions, and to live self-

controlled, upright and godly lives in this present age, while we wait for the blessed hope—the glorious appearing of our God and Savior, Jesus Christ, who gave himself for us to redeem us from all wickedness and to purify for himself a people that are his very own; eager to do what is good.

The picture Paul uses in this verse comes out more clearly in Greek than in English. He says that grace is our "pedagogue." In Paul's day, a pedagogue was an educated servant hired by wealthy families to tutor their children and train them in the knowledge and skills they needed in order to become successful adults. Training included everything from academics (grammar, logic, and rhetoric) to athletics and the arts. One of the most famous pedagogue-student relationships of the ancient world occurred in Macedonia when King Philip hired Aristotle to train his son Alexander the Great.

According to this text, grace is the servant God has assigned to train us in godliness. But surely this is a mistake! Isn't it the Law that tells us to say no to godlessness and worldly passions? After all, it is the law that gives us rules to obey and strict standards of behavior to follow. But Paul is absolutely right in saying that grace is our pedagogue. The Law is not a very good tutor. Simply telling us not to do something does not help us to not do it. In fact, it actually increases sin (Galatians 3:16). This was illustrated vividly at a resort in Galveston, Texas. The hotel was built in such a way that rooms facing the Gulf of Mexico had balconies that stretched out over the water. From this vantage point a person could actually go fishing in the Gulf from their balcony. The problem was that people kept breaking things and hurting people as they reeled in the fish they caught. To combat this problem the hotel management posted signs in every room telling people NOT to fish from the balcony. The problem became epidemic. People who would not have thought of fishing from the balcony suddenly thought it was a great idea! Finally, one of the junior managers suggested that they take the signs out of the rooms. With no other changes than this, the problem gradually disappeared.

Some people think that Christians need law to keep them under control and fear that grace will lead to a license for sin. But the opposite is actually true. Grace creates an environment of unconditional love. Grace teaches us that we are God's children and that sin is beneath us. Grace teaches us that we are invited to a divine romance and that sin is cheating on the most wonderful person in the universe with the most despicable being in the universe. Grace teaches us that we are saints and that when we live righteously we are acting like ourselves. The law teaches us that we are sinners and that when we sin we are acting like ourselves. Grace teaches us that we are already complete in Christ. The authors of an excellent book on grace titled, *True Faced*, put it this way:

> God is not interested in changing you. He already has. The new DNA is set. God wants you to believe that he has already changed you so that he can get on with the process of maturing you into who you already are. Trust opens the way for this process—for God to bring you to maturity. If you do not trust God, you can't mature, because your focus is messed up. You're still trying to change enough to be godly (*True Faced*, 45).

In his book *Classic Christianity* Bob George tells the following story, illustrating how God's grace is meant to be an incentive toward godliness.

> Imagine that you owned a fine cafeteria. One day, you hear this tremendous commotion out in the alley where the garbage dumpsters are. You open the back door to see what's going on, and you see the most pitiful-looking human being you have ever seen in your life—me—fighting with several stray cats over the food scraps in the dumpster. I am a virtual living skeleton. It's obvious that I am living on the edge of starvation, and probably have been for a long time. There is nothing about me to provoke liking or affection in you, but you are moved to pity.
>
> "Hey, hey!" you say. "I can't stand to see you eating garbage like that. Come into my cafeteria and eat."
>
> "But I don't have any money," I reply.
>
> "It doesn't matter," you say. "My chain of restaurants has done very well, and I can afford it. I want you to eat here every day from now on, absolutely free of charge!"
>
> You take my arm and lead me inside the restaurant. I cannot believe my eyes. I have never seen a cafeteria line before. With huge, unbelieving eyes I stare at the spread; vegetables … salads … fruits … beef … fish … chicken

…cakes …pies …In my wildest dreams, I have never even imagined that such things could be.

I look at you intently. "Are you saying I can eat *anything* I want?"

"Yes, anything."

"Really, *anything* I want?" I ask again.

"Yes, I said anything you want," you answer.

Then slowly, with a gleam in my eye, I ask, "Can I have some *garbage*?"

What would you think of me? You would think I was insane, wouldn't you? In the face of all that delicious food, all I can think of to ask is whether I can eat garbage. But that is exactly how I feel when people ask me if they can sin because they are under grace! (135-136, italics in the original).

THE PRACTICES OF A DEEPER WALK

To keep things simple, we will explore four practices that flow from and reinforce a grace perspective on life. These practices can be clearly seen in the life of Joshua. If anyone understood that his life was lived in the context of war, it was Joshua. He was chosen by God, and anointed by God's Spirit to lead Israel into battle in order to claim their inheritance in the Promised Land. His experience provides an excellent model of how to live a victorious Christian life. Israel's time in the wilderness can be thought of as their boot camp. It was God's time for training them to fight the battles they would face in the land of Canaan. Notice, however, that there is no record of them doing any real training for war. The Israelite camp probably did not look like a Samurai village with each man spending hours every day honing his skills as a warrior. On the contrary, Israel had only one battle strategy: Do things God's way and count on God to show up! There was no plan B. There was no backup strategy if God did not come through. Israel was to seek God, listen to His instructions, obey what He said, and watch what happened—Seek, Listen, Obey, Watch—S. L. O. W.

When Joshua followed this pattern, Israel always won! Now that is remarkable. It means that there is no such thing as a battle you cannot win, if you will seek, listen, and obey. There may be battles that God does not want you to fight (just as God did not want them to fight the Philistines just after they came out of Egypt), but you will not know that unless you seek God and listen for His guidance. Doing things God's way does not mean that you will never have battles, nor does it mean that every battle will be quickly and easily won (e.g., consider David's long struggle with Saul), nor does it mean that you will not suffer. God will lead you into battle time and again because it is the only way to develop the faith that produces endurance.

When Joshua did not follow this pattern, he had problems. He was defeated at Ai. He was deceived by the Gibeonites ("The men of Israel sampled their provisions but did not inquire of the Lord" 9:14). But he was never disowned by God. He was never abandoned or forsaken, even in failure. Instead, he was reminded to get back to the basics of seeking, listening, obeying, and watching.

The next several chapters of this book will be devoted to four essential practices we must build into our lives if we are to experience a deeper walk with God. To help us remember these we will use the hiking analogy described in chapter one.

The Backpack = Seeking God

The Bible, Water Bottle, and Journal = Listening to God

The Walking Stick = Obeying God

The Binoculars = Watching God and the enemy

These key ideas also spell the word SLOW: seeking, listening, obeying and watching. It is an appropriate word since we need to learn how to slow down if we are going to seek God and hear His voice.

THE THEME OF CHRONICLES

The theme of the book of Chronicles is seeking God. The primary Hebrew word for seek (*baqash*) is used more often in Chronicles than the rest of the Old Testament combined. The basic meaning of the word is to ask for something. We seek God when we ask Him to act or to speak, to provide power or wisdom. Early in Asa's reign the prophet Azariah told him, "Listen to me, Asa . . . the LORD is with you when you are with Him. If you seek him, he will be found by you, but if you abandon him, he will abandon you" (2 Chronicles 15:2). This warning embodies the thesis of First and Second Chronicles. The combined books are essentially a case study on the lives of the kings who sat on David's throne that asks just one question: "Did this king seek the Lord or did he abandon Him?" Depending on the answer to that one question, you can tell whether the battles the king is called to fight will end in victory or defeat and whether his reign will end in glory or infamy. The pattern is so consistent that it creates what I call a "duh" factor for the reader. After a while, as you read the stories, you start saying to yourself, "Duh, what did they think was going to happen!" The repetition of this pattern drives home just how central the idea of seeking God is meant to be to our lives.

Asa's life illustrates the pattern in Chronicles. At the beginning of his reign Asa rid Judah of its idols and made a vow to seek the LORD. As a result God gave the land peace for many years. That peace was threatened when an enormous army from Africa invaded Judah. Vastly outnumbered, Asa sought the Lord saying, "Yahweh, there is no one like you to help the powerless against the mighty. Help us, O Yahweh our God, for we rely on you, and in your name we have come against this vast army. O Yahweh, you are our God; do not let man prevail against you!" (14:11). As you might expect, the Lord gave him an overwhelming victory that day, and afterward Asa led all of Judah into a covenant to seek the Lord (15:12). Peace and prosperity returned to the land. However, in the last years of Asa's life his heart changed. His wealth and success made him proud. When a new threat rose up against him, he did not seek the Lord. Instead, he sought the help of a pagan king, Ben-Hadad. When a prophet rebuked him and tried to remind him of his vows, Asa threw that prophet in prison. Guess how Asa's life ended?

> In the thirty-ninth year of Asa's reign, he was afflicted with a disease in his feet. Though his disease was severe, even in his illness he did not seek help from the LORD, but only from the physicians. Then in the forty-first year of his reign, Asa died and rested with his fathers (16:12).

SEEKING AND ASKING

To seek God is to ask Him questions and look to Him for solutions to our problems. This is why the end of each chapter in this book includes a list of questions to guide you in seeking God about matters of the heart. We seek God when we ask Him for wisdom to guide us on our journey or power to solve our problems. The assumption in seeking God is that He wants to answer. When the kings of Judah sought Him and asked for wisdom, He often sent a prophet with an answer. Today, when we ask for wisdom, God's Spirit within us guides us to the wisdom we seek. Sometimes He speaks directly to our hearts. Sometimes He speaks through the Scriptures. Sometimes it is through other people or through life's circumstances. When there is a delay in hearing from God, we may need to get more serious about our asking. We may need to fast. Daniel waited for three weeks for an answer to his questions (Daniel 10).

In seeking God, one of the patterns I try to follow is to ask God to fix problems, then show me what role if any, He wants me to play. I used to ask God to *help me* fix problems, but I've discovered that things generally go better if I simply give the problems to Him to fix. Sometimes, that is all I need to do and He takes care of the rest. Other times He gives me something to do. In the Old Testament God often told people to stand and watch while He fought their battle for Him (as at the Red Sea). At other times, He gave people specific instructions for battle (as at Jericho).

The pattern can be seen clearly in the book of Joshua. When Israel came to the Jordan, Joshua sought the Lord, received instructions, obeyed, then watched God part the water. When they came to Jericho, he sought the Lord, listened to God's instructions, obeyed, and watched God knock down the walls. But when Israel came to Ai, Joshua did not seek the Lord, thus he could not listen, he could not obey, and he did not see God act. They did their own demographic research, formed their own battle plans, and then blamed God because the plans didn't work.

SEPARATING FROM THE ROUTINES OF LIFE

Let's face it. It is hard to carve out time for the important things in life. It was hard enough just to find time to read this book! Separating from the routines of life is really about building new routines into our lives. If you are like me, you may be panicked at the very thought of trying to build a good habit into your life. You know how often you have failed at such noble pursuits, and the thought of trying again seems pointless. I must confess that this has been a stumbling block for me. I fall quite easily into the performance mindset of fearing what God will think if I do not follow through on my commitment. As a result the idea of regular quiet times with God can become a duty that I dread. What helped me was to change my entire approach to connecting with God. I began by thinking of my time with Him as a date. It was hard at first because I had such high expectations. I was afraid that if God didn't speak to me, it meant that I was doing something wrong. I wanted every encounter to be a dramatic experience. Satan was trying to rob me of my time with God by turning it into a performance event. Once I realized this, I tried to take the pressure off of myself to do everything just right and learn to enjoy each experience for what it was.

With that in mind, let me give you a place to start.

Start by scheduling a weekly date with God. Put it into your calendar. Decide where you will go to meet with Him. Will it be the park? Your closet? A quiet chapel? Somewhere out in nature? Write the time and place into your calendar. Using that anchor point on your calendar, make it your goal to connect with God every day. Ask Him to show you how to do it. After all, this is a two-way relationship. He wants to meet with you even more than you want to meet with Him. After you have done this for a few weeks, schedule a whole day or an afternoon or evening with no other agenda than to spend time with God. Ask Him to show you how to do this and what He wants it to look like. Then go with whatever your heart tells you.

When I first began trying to schedule relational connection times with God, I picked two locations to meet with Him. One was a nearby park. I would walk the trails singing songs and meditating on Scripture then find a place to read my Bible and write in my journal. The other was the back room in the upstairs of our house. Soon I began to associate these places with seeking God, and a habit began to form.

I am a fan of John Maxwell's leadership books and have often marveled at what he has been able to accomplish. However, it wasn't until I read his book on prayer that I got the full picture of the secret of his success. As a freshman in college, John established the habit of spending time alone with God in the same place at the same time each day. He would bring his Bible and a notebook and spend an hour with God praying and listening. That practice became a lifelong habit with John and formed a relational foundation with God on which the superstructure of his leadership activity could be built.

Recently I developed the following acrostic to help me get focused at the start of each day.

S. Seek God first

T. Touch someone's heart (starting with my wife!)

A. Attack my day (have a "to do" list done the night before)

R. Remember who I am (and act like myself)

T. Tackle the tough stuff first

I don't follow it perfectly, but it helps to keep me focused on what is really important. It should make my wife happy, too!

CYCLES AND SEEKING

Have you ever wondered why God designed time to pass in cycles? Think about it. God made the earth spin on its axis so that we experience an evening and a morning every day. He gave us a Sabbath every week. He made the moon revolve around the earth so that we would have a new moon each month. He made the earth revolve around the sun so that we would have a new year with each revolution. God didn't have to design the world this way, but He did. Why? Well, at least one of the reasons is that He designed time to pass in cycles is because each new cycle is a reminder to seek Him.

The ceremonial law in the Old Testament is laid out according to this cycle. Every evening and morning there was a sacrifice. Every Sabbath was a day of rest. Every new moon special sacrifices were offered. Every year special festivals were celebrated in their season (2 Chronicles 8:12-13).

I do not think it is an accident that God made sunrises and sunsets so spectacular. Their beauty and grandeur call us to worship. They are reminders to set aside time to seek God through the practice of spiritual disciplines.

Bill Hybels, the founding pastor of Willow Creek Community Church, describes his decision to develop a more disciplined approach to prayer in his book *Too Busy Not to Pray.*

> Prayer has not always been my strong suit. For many years, even as senior pastor of a large church, I *knew* more about prayer than I ever *practiced* in my own life. I have a racehorse temperament, and the tugs of self-sufficiency and self-reliance are very real to me. I didn't want to get off the fast track long enough to find out what prayer is all about.
>
> But the Holy Spirit gave me a leading so direct that I couldn't ignore it, argue against it or disobey it. The leading was to explore, study and practice prayer until I finally understood it. I obeyed that leading. I read fifteen or twenty major books on prayer, some old and some new. I studied almost every passage on prayer in the Bible.
>
> And then I did something really radical: I prayed.
>
> It has been twenty years since I began taking time to pray, and my prayer life has been transformed. The greatest fulfillment has not been the list of miraculous answers to prayers I have received, although that has been wonderful. The greatest thrill has been the qualitative difference in my relationship with God. (11-12. italics in the original)

SPIRITUAL EXERCISE

Daniel is one of my favorite Bible characters. To share with us the secret of his success, the Bible points to the fact that Daniel had committed himself to seeking God in prayer three times a day. He also practiced fasting and other disciplines. Daniel knew what it was to hear God speak. He saw angels and visions. He received revelations about the future. His perspective on God had to be affected by these experiences, and that perspective led him to be very disciplined in his practice of seeking God.

1. How does your perspective of God affect your practice of seeking Him?

2. Does being disciplined make God love you more? Obviously not. So, why is it important? What keeps it from being mere duty or some thing you do to try to earn God's blessing?

3. For the next month try to set aside at least half an hour each day to meet with God in the same place and at the same time. Use this time to read your Bible and talk to God about what is on your heart. Write thoughts in your journal that come to mind.

4. Memorize 2 Chronicles 16:9, "For the eyes of the Lord range throughout the earth to strengthen those whose hearts are fully committed to him." To be fully committed to God means that you have removed the idols from your heart. Ask God to show you if there are idols in your heart that need to be torn down.

DISCUSSION QUESTIONS

1. Why is it important to develop the practice of spiritual disciplines?

2. How would you describe the difference between legalism and grace?

3. How can you relate the idea of a backpack to what you have learned about seeking God?

4. How would you describe what it means to seek God?

5. How would you summarize the teaching of Chronicles on seeking God?

6. What was your #1 take-away from this chapter?

7. What changes were you challenged to make or what steps were you challenged to take this week?

8. Did you make any strides in your walk this week you would like to share with the group?

9 PRACTICE 2: LISTENING TO GOD

A few years ago, a friend of mine named Mark paid my way to go to a retreat with John Eldredge and the Ransomed Heart team at a beautiful camp near Buena Vista, Colorado, in the heart of the Rockies. I was very excited. Not only did I love the idea of going to the Rockies; I was a big fan of the books Eldredge had written, and I was going to go with my brother and my father. It would be the first trip I could ever remember taking with just the three of us "Warner men" together.

One of the first exercises given to us at the retreat was to take our journals, find a spot with a great view of the mountains, and ask God to speak to our hearts about a specific question. I was still relatively new at the idea of listening to God and a bit skeptical about what would happen. I did as I was told, however, and soon found a pretty place to sit and pray. About fifteen minutes into the experience I grew impatient. I closed my journal and said to myself, "I knew this wasn't going to work!" My thoughts quickly turned from listening to God to arguing with Him. Completely discouraged, I decided to go do something that had always "filled me up" when I felt down. I went to a basketball court in the center of the camp, and started shooting baskets. I used to play a lot of basketball (after all, I am from Indiana!), and I made my first several shots. Then, I started to think about it: "If I keep my elbow here, and cock my wrist like this, maybe I'll keep this high shooting percentage going." If you have ever played competitive sports, you know what happened next. I missed my next seven shots. It was then that the Spirit spoke to me. "Marcus," He said, "You live your whole life like this." I asked Him what He meant, and a conversation began in my heart. "You try to be perfect instead of living from your heart." He was right. And He had just given me a graphic lesson on what it looked like. "Do you want me to go back to my place in the hills and pray?" I asked. But the Lord seemed to say, "No, stay and play. But this time . . . from your heart." The next half hour was a lot of fun!

HEARING GOD'S VOICE

For years I had no expectation of ever hearing God's voice. To think I might hear Him speak once or twice in my life seemed like a dream. Hearing God's voice seemed like something that only happened to very advanced, spiritual giants. I viewed my task as mastering every biblical principle there was and filing it away in my mind so that I could always pull up the right principle for the right occasion. I imagined my head as a filing cabinet in which I tried to store all this knowledge so that I would always make wise decisions. I had not learned that, as Eldredge puts it, "you cannot master enough principles to address every situation you will meet." (Eldredge, *The Way of the Wild at Heart, p. 254).* I often heard missionaries and other Christians talk about how God told them this or led them to do that, but I assumed it was a metaphor for the strong feeling they had about what they should do. The idea that God wanted to speak to me sounded pretty subjective, and I frankly never expected to have that experience.

Since then I have learned that not every thought that enters your head is yours. Some thoughts come from the enemy to tempt you, and some come from the Spirit to guide you. Some people fear the idea of listening to the Spirit because they know people who take it to extremes. Spirit-led living doesn't mean that you don't get out of bed unless the Spirit tells you to do so or that you don't tie your left shoe unless the Spirit gives you clear guidance in that area. God made you in His image and set you free in Christ so that you cold learn to be yourself and live from your heart. He just wants you to understand that on a fairly regular basis He will put His hand on your shoulder and whisper, "This is the way; walk in it." Or, "This is not the way, avoid it" (Isaiah 30:3).

LEARNING TO LISTEN

One of the reasons I did not expect to hear God's voice is that I did not understand that God speaks to the heart. I kept waiting for an audible voice or an angelic visit. Since I had no category in my thinking for the idea that I should be listening for the Spirit's voice within, I had no idea how to go about it. In God's providence, I knew a pastor named Tim Thomas who had a reputation for hearing from God. This man was a friend of the family, so I sought him out and asked him how to begin listening to the Spirit's voice. He pointed me to I Corinthians 10:13 and said, "God promises to show you the way of escape when you are tempted. So, the next time you are tempted, stop and ask God to show you the way of escape. When the Spirit speaks to you, pay attention to what you hear, and train yourself to listen for that voice."

Well, it wasn't too long before I had a chance to practice. A few weeks later, I got into a conversation with a friend that quickly turned into an argument. I felt falsely accused about a matter in which I knew myself to be innocent. At that moment, I remembered the pastor's words and asked the Spirit to show me the way of escape. Immediately, it was like I entered a time warp. Things seemed to slow down, because I think God wanted to make sure I got this. The words of James 1:20 came to my mind, "Man's wrath does not accomplish God's righteous purposes." I had learned that verse in fifth grade and forgotten all about it. But the Spirit brought it to mind when I needed it most. Next, He reminded me of Proverbs 15:1, "A gentle answer turns away wrath." The Spirit then showed me the damage I would do to my relationship if I gave in to my anger. It would take months to repair the damage, and it would never really be the same again.

At that point, I had to make a choice: live in the Spirit or live in the flesh. My flesh desired to unleash my anger. It felt justified in doing so.

But the Spirit was counseling a different course, and it was unmistakably God's voice. So, I chose gentleness. I said to my friend, "Are you saying that this is entirely my fault?" Immediately, he began to back pedal and let me know that he was just venting, that he was upset with the situation, and that he was sorry he was taking it out on me. Everything ended up great!

Living in the Spirit doesn't mean that everything will always end up great. Sometimes people truly are evil and do very evil things. Living in the Spirit won't necessarily prevent that evil, but it will guide you through it and on to the other side. The Spirit wanted me to learn not just how to listen to His voice, but to see how often I create problems for myself that don't need to be there, if I would just listen to Him!

ITEMS FOR THE BACKPACK

In this chapter we will look at three ways of listening to God's voice. These three approaches are illustrated as items to put into our backpack. These items are a Bible (to represent biblical meditation), a journal (to represent listening from your heart), and a bottle of water (to represent fasting).

THE BIBLE

In some ways, the Bible is an ordinary book. In other ways it is anything but ordinary. The Bible is ordinary in that it is comprised of words written on a page that can be analyzed and interpreted in a variety of ways. This is the way it tends to be studied in most non-evangelical institutions. However, it is extraordinary in that it has the capacity to "come alive" when the Holy Spirit uses it to speak to our hearts.

The Spirit and the Scriptures provide an incredible "one-two-punch" to guide us into wisdom. The Spirit is the source of all wisdom. He is also the ultimate author of the Scripture, since it was "breathed out" by Him to holy men of God who were "born along" by His guidance (2 Timothy 3:16; 2 Peter 1:21). There is, however, a veil over the Scriptures that is only removed in Christ (2 Corinthians 3:14). It is the Holy Spirit who removes this veil by speaking to our hearts as we listen to what He is saying through His Word. With the Bible in our hands and the Spirit in our hearts, we truly have the "mind of Christ" to guide us into all wisdom (1 Corinthians 2:16).

Sadly, there are times when people use the Scripture without the guidance of the Spirit and do great damage. The Word of God is called the Sword of the Spirit, and it can be dangerous when mishandled. The Bible can actually become a weapon when used in the flesh. We see it all the time with people who give Christians a bad name by the way they attack people with the Bible. We also see it with people who mean well, but who add to the burden of wounded people by pouring out Scriptural principles when they need to be listening and showing the compassion of the Lord.

BIBLICAL MEDITATION

Biblical meditation is the practice of praying and listening while you read or think about a passage of Scripture. It is asking the Spirit to speak to you from what you read or memorize. The purpose of meditation is not to attain the final word on the interpretation of a passage. It is to hear the Spirit's application of the passage to your life. His primary objective is character formation and the development of intimacy with God.

I often recommend to people who are new at this to simply ask the Spirit to speak to you, then start reading until something "jumps off the page" at you. If you read something that seems important, start talking to God about it. Ask Him for insight and clarification about what He wants you to know. If possible, write your thoughts in a journal or a notebook.

Sometimes I go to the Bible with specific questions when I need encouragement or guidance. I don't always get answers right away. There is no magic formula for getting God to give you the information you want or the solution you crave. Simply opening the Bible and asking God to speak is not the answer to all your problems. But it is an important practice to cultivate that deepens your walk with Him, and He often does use it to give you guidance and comfort.

Not long ago I was really struggling emotionally. I was working on this book and had just taught a seminar with a major focus on the sacred romance we were born to enjoy, but I was feeling very down on myself. I asked God, "Am I really the apple of your eye? Do you really have a passion for intimacy with me, or have I just stepped in line with the latest Christian fad?" I opened my Bible at random, hoping for some confirmation and, I kid you not, these were the first words I read:

> Is not Ephraim **my dear son**, the child **in whom I delight**? Though I often speak against him, I still remember him. Therefore **my heart yearns for him**; I have **great compassion** for him" (Jeremiah 31:20).

I couldn't believe it. I was so stunned, I sat up and started to laugh, and said, "Okay God, thanks for the confirmation."

THE JOURNAL

The first person I heard talk much about journaling was Bill Hybels, the pastor of Willow Creek Community Church. In his book *Too Busy Not to Pray* he writes,

> My first journal entry began, "Yesterday I said I hated the concept of journals and I had strong suspicions about anyone who has the time to journal, and I still do, but if this is what it's going to take to slow me down so I can learn to talk and walk with Christ the way I should, I'll journal."

Bill follows a pattern when he journals. First he takes a page to recap the previous day. This helps him get focused and slow down. Then he writes out a prayer to the Lord. Finally, he asks God questions and listens for promptings from the Spirit.

Personally, I never did much journaling until my retreat with Ransomed Heart. As one of the exercises we were told to ask God to show us our true name. One of the insights the Lord gave me on that occasion was that my name embodied my calling. My name is Marcus Ward Warner. The name Marcus is Latin and means "warrior." At that time I had what you might call a "love/hate" relationship with spiritual warfare. God used this occasion to confirm to me that there was a call on my life to enter this battle and fight for people's freedom. Ward is my grandfather's name. He was a plasterer, perhaps the best in Iowa in his day. He worked on great projects, and I felt God was saying to me that He had called me to build something in the area of spiritual warfare for the sake of His kingdom, and to be diligent about it. Finally, we came to the name Warner. In the circles in which I had been raised my dad was one of the most important people I knew. He was the president of Fort Wayne Bible College and later a professor at Trinity Evangelical Divinity School. Everyone I knew respected and admired him. Below the surface, I had struggled most of my life with the feeling that at the heart level, I did not have what it took to live up to my name. That day in the mountains, tears came to my eyes as the Lord simply said, "Marcus, you have what it takes."

I wrote these insights into my journal that day and have referred to them often. Since that day I have filled many journals with arguments, confessions, and insights from my times spent with God.

The point here is not that you have to write things in a journal in order to be spiritual but that the Spirit does want to speak to you, if you will learn to seek Him and expect an answer. Answers, of course, do not always come on our time table. When I first started seeking God with the goal of hearing His voice, I would get frustrated if I didn't hear anything significant in the first fifteen minutes. Daniel once waited three weeks to hear God's reply to a question (Daniel 10:2-4)! My goal is to encourage you to embrace the idea that God does want to speak to you and to begin your own journey of waiting and listening for His voice. Each journey will be different and will teach you many lessons, not only about listening to God, but about life, about God, and about your heart.

THE WATER BOTTLE

The water bottle represents *fasting*. Fasting is a form of sacrifice. In the Old Testament when people wanted to show God that they were serious about their petition, they would bring a sacrifice. Such offerings were a practical symbol of humility and respect. They were an acknowledgement of God's superior position and their need of Him. Like prayer, sacrifices open doors in the spiritual realms that would otherwise remain shut.

There seems to be a law in the universe that some things will not happen apart from sacrifice.

Fasting is a means of petitioning God. It is also a vivid reminder of our separation from the world. When you are fasting, you become acutely aware that your normal routine has been broken. Every time you feel hunger, you are reminded of the things of heaven. It helps you set your mind on things above and creates an atmosphere that keeps God in the forefront of your thoughts.

Before I started Deeper Walk Ministries, I was challenged by my friend Saji Lukos, the founder of Reaching Indians Ministries International (RIMI), to spend two days in fasting and prayer in order to confirm God's call. During that time my wife received clear guidance from the Spirit when she was awakened during the night and eventually wrote down several pages of insights that were prompted by the Spirit. My two days of fasting came and went with no clear word from the Lord. However, the day after the fast as I began to read my Bible, the Spirit began to speak.

My wife, Brenda, had left earlier in the day to go to see a family member in Ohio, and the last thing she had said to me was, "Marcus, we can do this." I thought her wording was unusual, so it stuck in my mind. Normally, she would say, "With God's help we can do this," or "If it is God's will we can do this." But to simply say, "We can do this," made an impression on me. You can imagine my reaction when, later that night, I read these words: "Then Caleb silenced the people before Moses and said, 'We should go up and take possession of the land, *for we can certainly do it!'*" (Numbers 13:30). It felt like God was speaking directly to me through these words. As I kept reading, I received stronger and stronger confirmation that God was calling me to launch this new ministry to the point that I felt I would be in a state of sin and rebellion if I refused.

This story contains elements of all three ways in which God speaks to us. I fasted, I meditated on Scripture, and I journaled what I felt the Spirit was saying to me. Later, I came up with a checklist of five leadings the Spirit gives when He is calling you.

S.   Speaks—The Spirit speaks to you and plants the dream in your heart

C. Confirms—The Spirit confirms what He has said through others

O. Opportunities—The Spirit opens doors that provide opportunities to serve

P. Provides—The Spirit provides the resources necessary to continue in the work

E. Enlarges—The Spirit enlarges the effectiveness of your ministry

There was a time when I thought that hearing God's voice was only for the super-spiritual. But I have come to realize that He wants it to be a normal part of life—a daily experience—and that if I will train my heart to listen, there is much He wants to say.

At the heart of a deeper walk with God is the practice of listening to His voice. Madame Guyon, a French Christian who was imprisoned for her faith, developed a deep and intimate connection with God in the solitude of her prison cell. People came to her from all over the land to learn the secret of her intimacy with Christ. In response, she wrote these words:

> Your spirit instructs your soul that, since God is more present deep within you, He <u>cannot</u> be found anywhere else. Henceforth, He <u>must</u> be sought within. And He must be enjoyed there alone. ... By moving into that inmost sanctuary again and again, you will finally become so established in your conversation that it becomes natural, even habitual to live in the Presence of God (Guyon, *Union with God*, pp. 1-2, emphasis in the original).

Isn't that our goal? Life in God's presence! It is not something that comes naturally. It is going to take practice.

SPIRITUAL EXERCISE

One of the most dramatic accounts of listening to God's voice comes from the life of the prophet Elijah. Discouraged that his victory at Mount Carmel had not led to national revival and afraid of Jezebel's wrath for his destruction of the priests of Baal, he fled to Mount Sinai. There God sent an earthquake, a fire, and a mighty wind; but when God finally spoke, it came as a "still small voice." That voice still speaks today.

1.   Schedule some time this week to ask God questions and listen for His answers.

2.   Memorize Galatians 5:13, "So I say, live by the Spirit and you will not gratify the desires of the flesh." Journal about what you have learned so far about what it means to live in the Spirit.

DISCUSSION QUESTIONS

1.   Can you identify the three items that fill the back pack and what they represent?

2.   Share your journey of learning to listen to God's voice?

3.   Did you listen? Did you do or say what was revealed? Why or why not?

4.   What gets in the way of listening to God's voice?

10 PRACTICE 3: OBEYING GOD

Bill Gillham, author of *Lifetime Guarantee*, tells a story that helped me get a really good picture of how the process of listening and obeying works. He calls it "the closet door story." Like many couples, he and his wife Anabel did not always agree on how to run things in the house. For example, his wife liked the closet doors in the house kept closed because it made things prettier. Bill liked to leave them open because it was more efficient. One day, he went to his bedroom to get a spring jacket out of the closet. He left the door open and headed down the hall. About half way down the hall he heard two clear, distinct words in his head say simply, "The door." He ignored the thought and kept walking, but once again he heard, "The door." So, he stopped. He recognized that the Holy Spirit was trying to get his attention. In describing the situation later, he said, "It had to be the Holy Spirit. Let's face it. It wasn't the power of sin!" He was at a crossroads, or what he calls "a mini cross." A mini cross is a fork in the road, where the devil is tempting us and the Spirit is guiding us, and we have to make a decision. Will we crucify our flesh and live for God, or will we quench the Spirit and walk in the flesh? That day Bill chose to obey. He said, "Lord Jesus, I am happy to serve you by offering myself to you to close the closet door for my wife." Then, he went back and closed the closet door.

Notice that the Spirit did not take control of Bill and make him obey. A Spirit-controlled life is not a mystical experience in which we literally lose control of our lives. The Spirit guided Bill. Because he had trained his heart to recognize the Spirit's voice, he was able to obey.

In telling the story Bill went on to observe that there are many times when we close closet doors in the flesh. How many times have we stomped back to the room and slammed the door shut, thinking to ourselves, "Stupid door! Controlling wife! There, I hope she's happy!" Or, we shut the door thinking, "Maybe if I do this for her now, she'll do something for me later?!" The flesh is very capable of putting on the appearance of righteousness without it coming from the heart.

The idea of mini-crosses has helped me recognize moments in my life when the Holy Spirit is trying to get my attention. Several years ago, I started looking at temptation as a mini-cross. I ask God to show me the way of escape so that by the Spirit I can put to death the misdeeds of the flesh. Not only do I ask God to show me the way of escape, I have begun to ask God to use the mini-cross as a teaching moment to show me why my flesh is so weak in that particular area. It is often an opportunity for God to show me an area in which wounds, lies, and vows have developed a stronghold or at least a distinct flesh pattern.

When a cart goes down a muddy path, it forms ruts. If this happens repeatedly or on a very muddy day, it can develop extremely deep ruts from which it is all but impossible to get free. This is a good picture of a flesh pattern. It is a place in my life that has been trained by trauma and repetition to respond in a fleshly way that is often very destructive, both to me and to the people around me. These ruts can get so pronounced that some refer to them as "flesh highways." Victory in such an area takes more than self-discipline. It often requires getting to the roots of the problem so that God can work through healing, deliverance and mental reprogramming. It is all part of living in the Spirit, and it begins with inviting God to begin peeling back the layers of self-deception that have been covering up some dark place in our hearts He wants to touch.

The difference between obedience as performance and obedience as humility is relationship. If I am "closing closet doors" in order to earn acceptance from God or praise from men, then I am doing it as performance. But if I am "closing closet doors" as an act of worship to the Lord, that is "walking humbly with my God."

THE GREAT COMMISSION AND OBEDIENCE

In the Great Commission (Matthew 28:18-20) Jesus said that we are to make disciples by baptizing people and teaching them to do what? To obey! To obey what? To obey everything he commanded! As Christians we have become disciples of a master who expects to be obeyed. The essence of discipleship is bowing the knee to a master. We kneel before the Lord Christ for two main reasons. First, his authority is absolute. He is the master; we are the servants. He is the teacher; we are the students. He is the king; we are the subjects. Second, His commands are wise. They lead to the good life our hearts desire. We may not always see how it all works, but we trust Him that, if we obey, He will work everything out for our good in the end.

To obey requires humility. It means that you must acknowledge that someone else has the authority to tell you what to do. Rebellion is born out of the arrogance that says, "No one is going to tell me what to do!" Cultivating the practice of obedience requires us to cultivate a spirit of humility. Most parents know the frustration of having a child with an unteachable spirit. Their pride hardens their hearts and closes their ears. Many prophets were given the thankless job of bringing God's message to arrogant, unteachable people whose hearts were hard and whose ears were closed.

The humility that leads to obedience is not the sort that is introspective and self-critical. It is the humility that knows how to submit to authority and accept criticism without becoming defensive. This is only possible when life stops being all about you. Humility is one of the defining qualities of maturity. It means you are free to be yourself because you aren't always thinking about yourself.

The Great Commission teaches us two very important lessons about obedience. (1) Obedience does not earn us a relationship with God. As Christians our relationship with God is founded on the finished work of Christ that purchased us for God. On the basis of that finished work we are invited into a relationship with God that is defined by the New Covenant. To be under that covenant is to be "in Christ." And all who are in Christ are pardoned from sin, adopted into God's family, made citizens of God's kingdom, and granted a new title—they are saints. The ceremony that celebrates our entrance into a new covenant relationship with God through Christ is baptism. Thus, baptism is the sign that we have renounced Satan, his kingdom, and his ways and embraced Jesus as our Lord, His kingdom as our primary citizenship, and His ways as our rule for life. It marks our entrance into the New Covenant.

Obedience has nothing to do with this. No one earns their way into the New Covenant. Nor do we maintain our place in the covenant through works. It has been provided by grace, and it is both received and maintained by faith (1 Corinthians 15:2). This faith, however, is not a mere intellectual acknowledgement that Jesus is the Son of God. It is a faith that leads to action. It leads to renouncing the ways of the world in order to take up our cross daily and follow our master. The first part of the Great Commission stresses the importance of baptism, which roots our relationship with God in grace.

(2) Obedience earns rewards from God. Paul described the relationship between grace and good deeds in I Corinthians 3:10-15. Jesus is our foundation. As long as we are "in him" we are secure and will be saved even if it as one who barely escapes the flames. On this foundation of grace, we are to build with good works. Our obedience does not make us more secure, but it does root us more deeply in Christ, and it achieves for us eternal rewards. The point here isn't to figure out what all of these rewards are. The point is that obedience is the natural fruit that flows from an intimate walk with God. It is not the foundation on which that relationship is based.

Obedience, therefore, is not the key to salvation, but it is the key to bearing fruit and experiencing blessing. "Do not be deceived," Paul wrote, "God is not mocked. What a man sows is what he will reap. He who sows to his flesh will from the flesh reap destruction. He who sows to the Spirit, from the Spirit will reap eternal life" (Galatians 6:8). All of this gets fuzzy when we start to think that our performance (how well we obey) is the foundation of our acceptance with God. Many of us worry that we have so disappointed God by our performance that He does not really accept us any more. This keeps us from pursuing intimacy with Him. After all, who wants to be transparent and vulnerable with someone who is disgusted with your weakness? Many of us are so used to receiving conditional love at a human level that we cannot conceive of receiving unconditional love at the divine level. God accepts us on the basis of the grace provided by the finished work of Christ. That acceptance is not conditional on how well we perform.

THE IMPORTANCE OF INTIMACY

A heart-focused journey is centered in a relational connection with Christ and not just a performance connection with Him. This was driven home to me one day when I was walking down the hall of the church where I served as senior pastor. My thoughts drifted to an image of an open field. In the middle of the field was a large boulder. I was tempted to dismiss the image as a daydream and refocus on my next project, when something inside seemed to say, "Look a little closer." I could see the picture in my mind the way a person can see a day dream. As I looked, I could see someone sitting on the boulder. I thought it was Jesus. There was a well-worn dirt path around the rock that formed a perfect circle. I soon noticed that there was little boy running on the path. Now and then he would look up at Jesus as if to say, "Look at me! Am I doing a good job?" Then, as clear as could be, I heard the words, "You know, Marcus, any time you want to stop running and climb up here, we could spend a little time together!"

God had captured the story of my life with a simple image that left an indelible impression. I was running in circles on the path of performance and missing out on the satisfaction and peace that come from enjoying a relationship with Him. I went straight to my office, closed the door, and spent a few minutes enjoying Jesus! I can't tell you what a difference it made in my day!

SPIRITUAL EXERCISES

Cain and Abel is the classic story of an obedient son and his rebellious brother. Abel had a teachable spirit. He had respect for authority and did things God's way. Cain, on the other hand, had a proud, rebellious spirit. When God corrected him, he was too proud to listen. He lacked a teachable spirit. Even God couldn't tell him what to do!

Examine your heart. Do you remember a time when you exhibited a proud, unteachable spirit? Or, a rebellious spirit that rejected authority? Or perhaps a defensive spirit that did not allow you to act like yourself in the face of criticism? Ask God to bring them to your mind and take steps to be F.R.E.E. Forgive those who provoked you. Repent of your attitude and actions. Eliminate behaviors still rooted in pride and rebellion, and evict the enemy who gained ground from your sin.

1. The next time you are tempted; stop, listen, and obey then watch and write down in your journal what happens.

2. Take off your mask with God. Bring your sin, fear, shame, anger, whatever to God. Trust Him that He will not reject you because of them. Don't rededicate yourself to trying harder to stop sinning. Invite God to Let Him put His arm around you and receive His love in the midst of your failure. The goal of the Christian life is not to be perfect, but to let yourself be loved by God so that your capacity to love and to love other imperfect people grows to be like Christ's.

3. Take off your mask with someone you trust. Share about your struggles and ask them to pray with you.

DISCUSSION QUESTIONS

1. What role does faith play in accepting God's love for us?

2. How does one's motivation to obey God change with one's view of God's character?

3. Which is the stronger motivation to obedience—law or love? Why?

11 PRACTICE 4:
WATCHING THE ENEMY

In the popular Star Wars series of movies George Lucas introduces us to warrior priests known as Jedi. These highly disciplined warriors learn the ways of "the Force," which is portrayed as a neutral power source created by the energy of life that emanates from every living thing. In classic pagan tradition, the Jedi learn secret arts in order to "tap in" to this energy and harness its power to levitate objects, control the weak minded, and manipulate the world around them. Modeled after Buddhist priests and practitioners of the martial arts, the expertise of these knights in using the Force makes them almost invincible in battle. If you have ever seen the movies, you can imagine how absurd it would be to think of a Jedi going into battle without using the Force! Just picture Obi-wan (a Jedi) meeting Anakin (a Jedi turned bad) and trying to fight him without using the Force. It would be a massacre. Yet I wonder how many Christians go into battle every day against a very real and potent spiritual enemy with no idea of how to "use the Spirit." (Technically, we do not "use" the Spirit, we submit to him and do things his way so that his power can flow through us.) We are reduced to fighting spiritual battles in the flesh.

In a sense, we are "Christian Jedi." But rather than tapping into a counterfeit occult power, we connect to the real thing. Yet how many of us have received the training we need to be confident in our ability to be "strong in the Lord and in his mighty power" (Ephesians 6:10)?

The symbol for learning to watch is a pair of binoculars. Just as binoculars have two lenses, so there are two areas in which we need to learn to watch. The first area is God Himself. We need to watch what God does when we seek Him, listen to His guidance, and do things His way. This is how we grow in faith.

WATCHING FOR GOD

Israel only had one battle strategy: seek God, listen to His directions, obey those commands, and wait for Him to "show up." If God didn't show up, they were doomed. Their faith that He would deliver them was the source of their confidence in battle. It is like the first grade kid facing down the third grade class bully out on the playground knowing that his two hundred pound, black-belt brother is just around the corner ready to step in at a moment's notice. It gives you confidence. This is what it is like to be "strong in the Lord." This is why the Psalms are filled with encouragements to declare to the nations what God has done. In telling the stories of those times that God has come through, our faith grows.

At Deeper Walk we have lots of stories of God's provision. Some are financial, like those times when money came in unexpectedly or at the last possible moment to keep the ministry afloat at a time when things looked pretty bleak. Some are relational, such as those times when a person was called or a contact was made that opened the door to unexpected ministry. But most come from the counseling room. There have been dramatic times when God showed up in a person's life to deliver and heal. Seeing God "show up" so many times gives you confidence for the future. It is also a reminder that you cannot presume upon God's blessing. You have to stay in relationship with Him by seeking, listening, and obeying.

Israel's battles at Jericho and Ai provide a classic example of how this works. Prior to Jericho, Joshua led Israel in seeking the Lord. They consecrated themselves, set up a memorial at the Jordan River, circumcised the males, and celebrated Passover. He also listened to God's instructions for the strategy to use in defeating Jericho. He led Israel to obey, then watched what happened. In our program-oriented, secularized approach to Christianity, our tendency would be to study the victory at Jericho, then write a manual on the importance of marching around walled cities thirteen times and shouting in order to conquer them. But that would miss the point, wouldn't it. The lesson from Jericho was the importance of listening and obeying in each new test. At Ai, Joshua did not seek or listen, and thus he could not obey. Had he sought God and listened, we can be sure God would have led him to deal with sin in the camp before the battle ever began. It would have saved lives.

WATCHING FOR THE ENEMY

If the first lens of our pair of binoculars represents watching for God, the second lens represents watching for the enemy. "Watch and pray" Jesus said, "so you do not fall into temptation" (Matthew 26:41). "Be alert and sober-minded," wrote Peter, "for your adversary the devil prowls around like a roaring lion, seeking someone to destroy" (1 Peter 5:7). Peter knew something about this. He had not listened to Jesus in the Garden of Gethsemane when he was told to watch and pray, thus he was not ready for the enemy attack. Satan had asked to "sift" Peter (Luke 22:31-32). This means that just as he had with Job, Satan had been granted special permission to attack Peter as a means of testing him. Peter failed the test, but that is not the end of the story. Satan wanted to sift Peter in order to destroy him. God allowed the sifting because he knew he could use it in Peter's life and overcome it in the end. God's sovereignty is such that by the time He was done with Peter, all Satan had accomplished by his attack was to help God make Peter into an even more formidable opponent. Peter learned a very important lesson from his experience of denying the Lord. He learned the importance of being alert and sober minded. He learned to watch and pray.

Here are a few tips when it comes to watching and praying.

1. Watch for the enemy when you are tired or bored. Like any lion who is hunting his prey, Satan goes after us when we are weakest. Satan came to Jesus in the desert when he was tired and hungry. Discouragement

overcame Elijah after a great battle with the enemy. David spied Bathsheba when he was supposed to be at war with his comrades in arms.

2. Watch for the enemy when you have just won a victory. Satan loves to snatch defeat from the jaws of victory, and he knows that pride goes before a fall. Imagine that you have just successfully faced a "mini-cross" in your life. You just overcame your fleshly desire to keep the closet door open and surrendered to Christ to allow him to use you to close the closet door for your wife. As you are walking down the hall feeling good about yourself for having handled things in the Spirit, you enter the kitchen just in time to have your wife scold you for failing to pay a bill you said you were going to pay over the weekend. All of a sudden you are faced with a second mini-cross. It would be natural (in the flesh) to respond defensively. After all, you just made a great sacrifice for her and instead of gratitude, you get attitude! Satan has just sprung a trap to try to snatch defeat from the jaws of victory. It is now up to you to act like the adult that you are, listen to the Spirit for the way of escape, and once again die to self and live in the Spirit.

The devil is not stupid. He knows that in order to kill the sheep, he has to separate the sheep from the shepherd. Our strength is "in the Lord." The entire focus of the Christian life is abiding in Christ. It is relational. When we are in intimate relationship with Christ, his life flows through us and we bear fruit.

3. Watch for the enemy in known danger zones. When I was just seven years old, I found a big box of porn magazines in my neighborhood. My friends (who were a couple of years older than I) and I hid them in the attic of my garage where we had a "fort" and used to go up there and look at them for hours. Eventually, the Spirit got a hold of me and I got rid of all of the magazines, much to the annoyance of my friends. I waited almost two years before I told anyone about my experience. At that young age, Satan managed to damage something in my heart, and seeds were planted that I have had to wrestle with at different times in my life. I have learned that I need to stay away from certain aisles in the book store and surfing the internet at night. It is too easy to rationalize what I am doing and allow myself to go to sites where I know there are probably pictures

of pretty girls.

Whether it is pornography or drunkenness or some other habitual problem, part of watching for the enemy is learning what his patterns are for attacking us and staying clear of danger zones where we know the enemy attack is most likely.

4. Watch for the enemy in flattering words. Pride loves the praise of men. It is easy for us to think of attack only as the temptation to darkness, but sometimes he comes to us as an angel of light. There have been false brothers, false prophets, false teachers, and false apostles in the church almost since it began. We need to remember that just because people are faithful participants at church doesn't mean that they are allies. Your enemies are not always those who oppose you. Often they are those who befriend you. You don't have to be paranoid, but Jesus warned us to beware of false prophets (Matthew 7) and Paul told the Ephesian elders that he was certain wolves in sheep's clothing would arise from within and threaten the church.

5. Watch for the enemy in your wounds, lies, and vows. Perhaps the most devastating tactic of the enemy is his success at planting lies in our hearts that warp our view of God and our view of ourselves. It is important for us to recognize how the enemy has attacked us over the years. What our wounds are, what the lies are that he has used against us, and what the vows are that we have made in response. There is almost always a pattern to his attack, and that pattern usually goes straight at our heart in a way that sabotages our ability to live in intimacy with God.

Early in my life, my heart's view of God was undermined by the enemy. It all began with a dream. I was about three years old and had just come home from a class at church in which a well-meaning but misguided teacher decided to tell her preschoolers about hell and how God would send us there if we didn't accept Christ. For the next two nights, I had very vivid nightmares in which I saw the terrors of a dark, fiery pit and felt the horror and almost psychotic desperation of what it would mean to be sent there forever. I woke up in a panic. Running to my mom's room, I asked, "What do I have to do to be sure that I never go to hell?"

Unaware of the full implications of my experience, she led me in a prayer to receive Jesus into my heart and the nightmares went away. For a long time, I thought that was the end of the story and that God had sent me the dreams so that I would receive Christ at an early age. But recently I have begun to see that the enemy sent me those dreams, not God. I have begun to realize that they were part of Satan's strategy to rob my heart of intimacy with God. As a result of my vision of hell, the enemy succeeded in planting a lie in my heart at a very early age that was reinforced in a variety of ways throughout my life. His lie was that God is the sort of person who tortures people unmercifully if they don't jump through the right hoops. Now, I would never have said that to anyone, but it was the message my heart embraced. The result was a vow unconsciously made that I would jump through God's hoops in order to avoid hell, but I could never really love Him. After all, who could love a sadistic God like the one painted for me by the devil. The fruit of this wound, lie, vow pattern was a divided heart. Was God good or was He bad? Was he angry with me or happy with me? Had I done enough to be sure I wasn't going to hell? How could I ever be good enough when I knew in my heart that I didn't fully trust Him? Such struggles about God rendered intimacy with Him virtually impossible. Over the years, the division in my heart grew worse, reinforced by various aspects of my life experience. Part of me loved God and wanted to please Him, and part of me feared God and wished that He didn't exist. It has only been in the last few years that I have realized how deeply ingrained this pattern of mistrust for God has been.

Knowing how Satan attacked me has helped me to see just how important intimacy with God is. If it wasn't, he wouldn't have worked so hard to keep it from happening. I am learning to recognize when the lies and vows related to past wounds are driving my behavior, and it is beginning to make a difference in the way I live. For me, the command to watch and pray has a lot do with learning to recognize the pattern of attack he has used against me all of my life to separate me from God.

You need to learn to watch and pray because the devil has a specific plan of attack designed just for you. John Eldredge made this very clear at the retreat I attended. He said that the enemy wants to "take you out" at the heart level and eliminate you as a potential threat. He attacks you because as a child of God who is made in His image you have the power to inflict incredible damage on his kingdom if you ever learn to walk in the kind of intimacy that allows the life of Christ to flow through you. Because of this you need to learn to recognize Satan's strategies and stay alert to his efforts to undermine your walk with Christ. Peter warns us to "be alert" as we watch for the enemy's attacks (1 Peter 5:8). Paul uses the same Greek word in 1 Thessalonians 5:6, when he urges us to "be alert" as we await the coming of Christ.

Just as a Jedi's power comes from the Force, our power in the Christian journey comes from our connection with Christ. It is as we abide in Christ that his life flows through us. As Jesus said, "Apart from me you can do nothing" (John 15:5). It makes sense, therefore, that our enemy would do whatever he can to rob us of that intimacy with Christ that leads to spiritual power and abundance. His schemes and methods are devoted to sabotaging our walk with Christ.

SPIRITUAL EXERCISES

Joseph knew what it was to watch for temptation. As the steward of Potiphar's house, the master's wife tried many times to seduce him. The pressure to give in had to be tremendous, even if there was no personal attraction involved. She was in a position of power over him and had the ability to ruin his life or even have him executed. Joseph's commitment to live as a person of character led to a commitment to watch and pray.

We live in an era in which a growing number of pastors and Christian workers have fallen into sexual sin. One of the reasons for this is that we often become so busy in ministry that we lose connection with our hearts. We are so busy doing and making sure we look good on the outside that our intimacy with God suffers. Bruce Wilkinson tells of a time in his ministry when he began to burn out. Things of the world started looking very tempting. He called a friend of his who said, "You're right on schedule, Bruce." Most successful Christian leaders begin their journeys with a great sense of dependence on God. Consequently, they pray regularly and desperately, and their walk with God is high. But as the years go by they become increasingly competent at what they do. Outcomes become more measurable and predictable and the ministry becomes mere work. Thus, as competence rises, intimacy tends to wane, and leaders become separated from their hearts.

One of the main reasons we need to watch and pray is to guard our hearts and protect our walk with God. We are asking for trouble, if we don't.

1. Ask God to open your eyes to areas of enemy attack in your life. Write down what He shows you and share it with someone you trust.

2. Ask God to open your eyes to area where He is at work in your life. Write down what He shows you and share it with someone you trust.

If you suspect that you have wounds, lies, and vows that are undermining your walk with God, talk to Him about them. Ask Him to begin showing you what your wounds are whether Type A or Type B. Take your journal to a quiet place and ask Him to show you the lies that were planted in your heart and the vows that are controlling your life. Begin seeking Him for answers and listening to the guidance of His Spirit to set a path for your healing. God may be waiting to talk to you about these things. You may even find that entering into your pain in this way is the gateway to the intimacy with God your heart has desired.

DISCUSSION QUESTIONS

1. Can you give an example of how a person "uses the Spirit" to win spiritual battles?

2. What kind of lies does Satan commonly plant in our hearts?

3. How would you put into words Satan's strategy to take you out of the battle?

4. Can you name the lie(s) Satan uses most against you?

5. What insight from this chapter meant the most to you? Why?

12 MATURITY DEVELOPMENT

We began this journey with a discussion of what it means to be mature and how many of us have holes in our maturity because of trauma in our past. This chapter could be titled "Next Steps" or "Where do we go from here?" I thought about developing five steps to this or four habits of that, but realized I really just have two closing suggestions:

BALANCE

During the 1970's my father had a five minute spot on the radio called "Keeping Your Balance." His basic premise was simple: "The Christian life is the exciting process of learning to keep your balance." He developed this thesis in two basic directions. He taught that it is important to develop a balance among your interests and activities such as art, athletics, music, reading, and the like. He also taught the importance of avoiding Satan's extremes. He believed that Satan introduces his lies in pairs in order to move us away from the biblical center of healthy living and into an unbalanced extreme. A classic example would be sexuality. There is a biblically balanced, emotionally healthy approach to sexuality that is satisfying and fulfilling. Satan wants to move us from that healthy place of balance to an extreme. He really doesn't care whether we go to the extreme of labeling all sexuality as evil or moving in the opposite direction of permissiveness and perversion – just so we "lose our balance." Either way the result is spiritual bondage that robs us of freedom, confidence, and often much, much more.

This balance principle can be applied to all sorts of issues. We can get out of balance in regard to music and entertainment, the time we spend at work, the food we eat, or the focus we place on our own physical and emotional health. The key to learning balance is finding a center. I like golf, and now and then I will pick up a book or a magazine on how to improve my play. In one book I learned that many professional players set aside special golf balls just for putting. They do this because, unlike most golf balls, these are perfectly balanced. This is crucial for good putting. A golf ball that is not perfectly centered won't hold a straight line. You can strike it perfectly, on exactly the right line at exactly the right speed and still miss the putt because an unbalanced ball won't hold its line. It will curve to the right or the left because it lacks a true center. People are no different. If our inner man is out of balance, we are going to have trouble staying on the "straight and narrow path."

I believe a centered life is about passion. To be passionate about something is to want it so badly that the suffering you endure to get it seems like a small price to pay for the reward at the end. Great love stories are about the passion that drives heroes to overcome great trials for the sake of their beloved. Athletes and artists often endure intense suffering for the sake of their passion. The apostle Paul embodies passion. For him life was simple: "To live is Christ. To die is gain." His passion for Christ led him to endure a range of suffering few of us could even imagine (2 Corinthians 11). Because of his passion, Paul found joy in the midst of his suffering, thus he could write, "Though outwardly we are wasting away, yet inwardly we are being renewed day by day."

The Greek word most often associated with passion is *epithumia*. It is the word used in the Greek version of the Ten Commandments that means "to covet." It is frequently translated as "lust" in the New Testament. But *epithumia* can also mean strong desire or passion in a good sense. Jesus said that he strongly desired (*epithumia*) to eat the Passover with his disciples. The point is that desires are often rooted in legitimate needs. Fleshly desires get twisted because we seek to meet those needs apart from God and look to the world to provide the protection and pleasure we desire.

Someone once said that Americans worship their work, work at their play, and play at their worship. I am afraid this is all too true. However, honoring God in all we do makes everything we do an act of worship. This was the secret of a monk named Brother Lawrence. He scrubbed pots and pans and did menial chores throughout the day, yet he had such a reputation for joy, peace, and love that people regularly sought to discover his spiritual secret. He did not spend hours in prayer each day as some— often unhappy—monks did who were trying to earn God's approval by their works. He did not study the Bible extensively. In fact, his life was nothing extraordinary when it came to the practice of the more obvious spiritual disciplines. His secret was found in the name of his classic devotional, *Practicing the Presence of God.* Brother Lawrence enjoyed God. He delighted himself in the Lord and experienced Him in everything he did. This connection with God was a perpetual source of joy that enabled him to treat others with grace and humility. It allowed him to be himself.

Balance in life comes from enjoying God's role in our work, our play, and our worship. Too often we leave God out of these things and do them in the flesh. Work becomes a burden. Play becomes an escape. Worship becomes an obligation. Life loses balance. We lose our passion. As a result, our hearts begin to leak joy.

The perspectives and practices taught in this book are intended to help you find and enjoy God in a way that brings to life the desires of the heart that will make you fully alive.

REDEMPTIVE RELATIONSHIPS

Relationships are the most fundamental part of life. This is because God, at the core of His being, is relational. God is love in a very tangible sense. Father, Son, and Holy Spirit live in a perpetual relationship of love in which the three are one. There has never been time when God has not been in relationship. There has never been a time when God was not displaying and enjoying love.

The very reason for our existence is our participation in this divine romance. That is why Satan works so hard to disrupt it. He doesn't want us to enjoy God or trust His love for us; so, as John Eldredge puts it, he targets our hearts with his arrows. In this fallen world who has heard of a heart that has not been broken? The story is told of a woman who came to Buddha hoping to find a cure for her dying son. He instructed her to bring him ten grains of rice, each one from a home that had not been touched by the suffering of death, and her son would be healed. It did not take the woman long to realize what the teacher was trying to teach her. Death and suffering afflict us all. It is simply part of life under the sun.

Life is a journey meant to be traveled with companionship. God's verdict that it is not good for man to be alone has not changed. We are meant to live our lives in relationship with God and our fellow-travelers. Is it any wonder then that most of our problems stem from relationships gone bad? Whether it is a parent-child relationship, a husband-wife relationship, or some other relational issue, most of our emotional baggage is rooted in some type of relational problem. This is why it is so important to invest in the development of redemptive relationships.

A redemptive relationship is an emotionally healthy connection with another person or group that gives you a place where it is safe to be yourself. Not only is role playing not required; it is not allowed. No masks are permitted to be worn. You are encouraged to be yourself.

One of the reasons dogs are so popular is that they always seem happy to see you. Their wagging tails and slobbery greetings seem to shout out, "Oh boy, oh boy, it's you!" And isn't that what we are looking for; someone who is happy to be with us? Some of us, convinced we will never find anyone who truly accepts us, have learned to hide. We all hide to some extent. It is even a healthy practice in many situations. Jesus knew who he was and wasn't afraid to be himself, but he didn't make himself vulnerable to everyone. He kept some things hidden, not out of shame, but out of wisdom. He was careful about who he opened up to. When he made himself vulnerable to his enemies, he did so strategically as an act of love, knowing it would cost him his life. Our problem comes when we hide for so long that we forget who we are and what it means to be ourselves. We start hiding even when we are with safe people. We hide from God because He doesn't feel safe. We hide from our spouses, our peers, and in the process it seems that there is no place where we can be ourselves.

Redemptive relationships are ones that are safe because people are happy to see you regardless of your performance. Such relationships give you a place to belong. They are rooted in a commitment that is often unstated to be an accepting person. No one is trying to fix the other person in a redemptive relationship, and no one is asking the other person to save them. It is just a place where it is okay to be yourself. Ideally, these relationships are formed in the home. Marriage and family are supposed to provide the ultimate in acceptance and belonging. Sadly, this is often not the case. The church is also meant to be a family in which people love one anther. It was Christ's number one commandment: "Above all else provide a safe place for people to grow and heal by loving one another." Unfortunately, we often elevate truth and justice above love. Thus, if people disagree with us, we excuse ourselves from loving them, or if people disappoint us, we excuse ourselves from loving them. This does not mean that we live without boundaries or that we never confront error. But we do so in love. Loving someone can be defined as doing what is good for them. That doesn't always means doing what they want. A safe place is not one in which you are never confronted with your failures and sins, nor is it one in which there are no consequences for bad behavior. It is a place in which confrontation and consequences are fair and honest and handled with our best interests in mind.

Although the church as an institution is not always a safe place characterized by love, it is generally from among true believers that we find people with whom to form healthy relationships that challenge us to grow in maturity.

CONCLUSION

I have a long way to go on my journey. Most of us probably do. I am beginning to realize how much of my life has been about pain avoidance, false expectations, and a burdensome view of Christianity that was molded by behavior-focused discipleship and the attacks of the enemy. It is out of this journey that I share with you some of the perspectives and practices that are beginning to chip away at the prison walls that have surrounded my heart. Don't get me wrong. I've had a great life by almost any standard. I have a great family, I get to do what I love, and I have had many wonderful experiences. It is just that I have lived most of my life separated from my heart, and I am beginning to realize why. Any walk with God is a redemptive walk. It's what God does. He restores and heals. He brings order out of chaos and speaks light into darkness. Along the way He blesses us and tests us and uses us to touch the lives of others.

I pray that this book will help you on your journey. I hope the lessons that have helped me go deeper in my walk will help you as well as you pursue a journey of the heart.

SPIRITUAL EXERCISE

When Jesus wanted a text that expressed his mission in life, He chose Isaiah 61. "The Spirit of the Lord is upon me, because He has anointed me to preach good news to the poor. He has sent me to bind up the brokenhearted, to proclaim freedom for the captives and release from darkness for the prisoners, to proclaim the year of the Lord's favor . . ." God is a redeemer. His specialty is reclaiming that which has been damaged. He has been bringing light to darkness and order out of chaos since the first day of creation. His heart of love for us is greater and more awesomely passionate to see good come our way (especially in the age to come) than we will ever know.

1. Take time to reflect on where your journey has taken you as you have worked through this book and these exercises. Where were you when you started? Where are you now? Do you see progress in identifying holes in your maturity or any movement toward healing and maturity in areas of brokenness?

2. Ask God to show you His next step for you. Write it out in black and white and share it with someone. Then take that step.

DISCUSSION STARTERS

1. How has this study impacted your life?

2. What insight from this or previous lessons has meant the most to you and why?

3. What are some of the obstacles that challenge your ability to live from your heart?

4. Share about a time in your life when you experienced the balance that comes from being centered in Christ. What contributed to that experience?

5. Have you ever experienced a redemptive relationship? How would you describe it? What made it "redemptive?"

6. How has your view of God and yourself been impacted by this study?

APPENDIX: APPLYING A DEEPER WALK APPROACH IN THE CHURCH

This information is placed in an appendix because it is not intended for small group discussion or as part of the discipleship material. It contains a series of suggestions for ways to implement a Deeper Walk approach to discipleship in the local church.

I. DEVELOP A DEEPER WALK CENTER IN YOUR LOCAL CHURCH

A Deeper Walk center is a place that connects people to the services offered by the church that relate to heart-focused discipleship. Such services include classes, small groups, resources, counseling, and personalized discipleship guidance. Such a center could be as simple as a booth in the lobby or as significant as a set of rooms devoted to discipleship and counseling. The purpose of the center is to develop a concrete means of promoting the practice of heart focused discipleship. It would be the gateway to some of the following services.

GUIDES. Guides are Christian workers who have been trained to lead others into an understanding of the core perspectives and practices set forth in this book. Any local church that wants to be successful in making disciples is going to need to make a significant investment into the development of such guides who can walk alongside people and mentor them in the ways of a deeper walk with Christ.

INSTITUTE. Small groups are not enough if you want to make disciples. You need to provide opportunities for in-depth training. A Deeper Walk Institute is one that is devoted to providing training in four key areas: (1) Bible -- including doctrine and church history (2) Discipleship -- instruction in Spirit-filled living and spiritual warfare (3) Counseling – training in identifying and overcoming the obstacles that sabotage maturity (4) Ministry – developing skills and strategies for ministering to others. Such an institute would provide a series of courses especially designed to develop leaders in the church who are capable of functioning as spiritual parents. A typical course might last 8-12 weeks with each session lasting 1 ½ to 2 hours. Sunday night is often a good time for such courses.

COUNSELING CENTER. One of the obstacles that keeps people from experiencing a deeper walk is their inability to find victory over the battles and baggage of life. Ideally, any guide should be able to walk someone through the basics of understanding their identity in Christ and taking them through the steps of forgiveness and repentance. But there are cases that require more training and experience than a typical guide is likely to have. For such cases it is good either to have a counseling center in the church or to partner with a trusted counseling center in the area.

RESOURCES. It is important to build a good set of resources that reinforce the commitment to heart-focused discipleship. By having a clear philosophy of discipleship, you can be more strategic and intentional about the types of resources you collect and avoid simply going with the latest fad.

II. DEVELOP A STRATEGIC PARTNERSHIP WITH DEEPER WALK INTERNATIONAL

Deeper Walk International wants to help you succeed in building mature believers and ministering to wounded hearts. We can do this in a variety of ways.

TRAINING EVENTS. A good way to start is to bring a training event to your church. A Deeper Walk event can awaken your church to the need for heart-focused discipleship and help you "jump-start" the process of building a team of guides who can minister effectively to others.

INSTITUTE FOR BIBLICAL COUNSELING. Deeper Walk International provides advanced training for those who want to go further in developing their ability to minister to hurting people. We provide courses in spiritual warfare, healing prayer, and specific issues frequently encountered in pastoral counseling.

RESOURCES. Deeper Walk offers a variety of books and resources that can be used individually, in classes, or in small groups to help you make disciples and develop leaders.

ASSOCIATION. As this book is being written, Deeper Walk International is in the process of developing an association that can help you stay networked with other churches, ministries, and Christian workers who embrace a heart-focused approach to ministry.

For more information about how to implement a heart-focused strategy at your church visit the website: www.deeperwalkinternational.org.